THE POCKET
DISASTER
SURVIVAL
GUIDE

WHAT TO DO WHEN THE LIGHTS GO OUT

HARRIS J. ANDREWS & J. ALEXANDER BOWERS

Skyhorse Publishing

Skyhorse Publishing books may be purchased in bulk at special discounts for sales promotion, corporate gifts, fund-raising, or educational purposes. Special editions can also be created to specifications. For details, contact the Special Sales Department, Skyhorse Publishing, 307 West 36th Street, 11th Floor, New York, NY 10018 or info@skyhorsepublishing.com.

Skyhorse® and Skyhorse Publishing® are registered trademarks of Skyhorse Publishing, Inc.®, a Delaware corporation.

Visit our website at www.skyhorsepublishing.com.

10 9 8 7

Library of Congress Cataloging-in-Publication Data is available on file.

ISBN: 978-1-60239-992-1

Printed in China

This book is dedicated
to all emergency professionals and
volunteers, public safety personnel,
relief workers and all those who just wade
in to help their neighbors during a crisis.
Thank you.

CONTENTS

INTRODUCTION

Every year, thousands of people throughout North America find themselves faced with an unexpected emergency. They face hurricanes, tornadoes, or simply a windstorm and loss of power. Suddenly, they find themselves depending upon their own means and abilities to stay comfortable or in the worst case, alive.

Our world has become dependent on complex, interlinked public services that provide the basic necessities of life. We light our homes with electricity from continent-spanning power grids. Clean water is delivered into our homes through sanitary underground pipes, purified of harmful organisms by regional treatment systems. Other vast systems carry away and purify our garbage and waste products. Complex transportation networks, powered by electricity and gasoline, move along rail and road systems to deliver food and other daily needs to distribution points near our homes. We store and cook our food with appliances powered by electricity or piped-in natural gas. The examples of our dependence on technology for the basics of existence are endless.

Our technological network can be fragile. A severe windstorm or even a minor glitch in the management of the power grid can cut off most of our sources of clean water, food, heat, and light. In the worst case, a major disaster—hurricane, tornado, earthquake, or winter storm—can wreck water, sewage, and power systems; disrupt communications and destroy homes, businesses, and transportation systems. You may have to sit in the dark for a few hours—but in the worst case, you may have to dig yourself out of the rubble and survive until help comes.

Getting along successfully during and after any disaster calls for a combination of preparedness, knowledge, and a minimum selection of the right supplies. *The Pocket Disaster Survival Guide* is a comprehensive and easy-to-use pocket guide to the basic information you need to handle a wide range of emergency situations. This book deals with survival and coping basics ranging from vital elements such as water, food, and personal safety to the know-how and equipment you need to make life bearable in the aftermath of a natural or man-made disaster.

Read this book ahead of time so that you can be prepared to make informed, well-considered decisions about the level of preparedness you need to keep safe during and after trying times. This book can be with you in the aftermath of a disaster, acting as a reminder of those things you need to know under stressful and confusing situations. Ultimately, the pocket guide will help you prepare for that moment when the lights go out.

1. EMERGENCY PREPAREDNESS

We usually don't want to wish trouble upon our-selves, but the possibility of facing a major or minor natural or man-made disaster is always present. It is always a good idea to learn how to protect yourself and cope with disaster by planning ahead; when disaster strikes you may not have much time to act. Take time to learn about the potential hazards that may occur in your region and find out about your community's disaster response plans and procedures for warning and evacuation. Above all, take basic, sensible precautions and learn what to do if you face an emergency.

EMERGENCY PLANS

Create a plan for the family.
- Find the safe locations in your home for each type of disaster you may have to face.
- Make sure all family members, including children, know how and when to call 911, police and fire, and post emergency telephone numbers near telephones.
- Discuss what to do about power outages and teach family members how to turn off the water, gas, and electricity at main switches when necessary.
- Pick two emergency meeting places: A place

near your home and a place outside your neighborhood in case you cannot return home after a disaster.

- Find out about your children's school emergency plan and monitor local media broadcasts for directions from local emergency officials' announcements about changes in school openings and closings. In cases where schools initiate shelter-in-place procedures, you may not be permitted to pick up your children; the school doors will probably be locked for safety.

FAMILY COMMUNICATION PLAN

In case family members are separated from one another during a disaster, create a plan for getting back together. Find an out-of-state relative or friend to serve as an emergency contact (it is frequently easier to call out-of-state than within the affected area) and be sure that everyone knows the name, address, and phone number of the contact. Make sure that every family member knows family and emergency contact numbers:

- ❑ 911, police, fire, hospital
- ❑ Alternate phone numbers or family members (work, cell, pager, etc.)
- ❑ Neighbors' names and telephone numbers
- ❑ Electric, gas, and water companies

EVACUATION PLAN

Plan ahead where to go and what to take with you if you are forced to leave. Making plans at the last minute is sure to cause panic and confusion. If community evacuation becomes necessary, local officials will provide evacuation warnings and instructions via local radio and television broadcasts. In some locations, other warning methods such as sirens or telephone calls are used.

Remember, it is vital to plan ahead. The amount of time you have to evacuate will depend on the type of emergency you face. In some potential disaster situations, a hurricane that can be monitored for example, you might have several days to prepare, but in other situations, such as a chemical release or flash flood, there may be no time to assemble even the most basic necessities.

HOUSEHOLD ESCAPE PLAN

In some emergencies, you may need to get out of your home fast. Work out an escape plan by drawing a floor plan of your dwelling that shows the location of doors, windows, stairways and items of large furniture. Show the location of emergency supplies—fire extinguishers, collapsible ladders, first-aid kits and utility shut-off points. Chart at least two escape routes from each room. Designate a place outside of the home where everyone should meet.

SAFETY SKILLS

- Learn first aid and take a CPR class. Your local American Red Cross chapter can provide this type of training and certification.

- Be sure that everyone knows how to use a fire extinguisher and where it is kept.
- Review potential disaster scenarios in your area and learn how to take personal protection measures—where to seek shelter, when to duck and cover.

DISASTER SUPPLY KITS

Review what disasters you might face and assemble any emergency supplies you might need to store in your household or for an evacuation. Store them in easy-to-find places and keep evacuation supplies in a portable container such as a backpack or duffle bag. Make sure you have the tools you need to deal with any emergency.

FIRE EXTINGUISHERS

Fire extinguishers are your first line of defense against fire. Selecting the proper extinguisher is important to ensure that you have the right kind for the expected type of fire and to reduce damage to valuables caused by extinguishing agents. Make sure everyone knows the location, use, and limitations of your fire extinguishers. Extinguishers should be checked and serviced once a year.

Selecting a Fire Extinguisher

Extinguishers are classified according to the type of fire for which they are suitable.

- **Class A:** Ordinary combustibles—wood, paper, cloth, and most plastics.

- **Class B:** Flammable liquids and gases—gasoline, oils, paint, lacquers, and greases.
- **Class C:** Live electrical equipment—extinguishing agent must be nonconductive.

Extinguishers also have a numerical rating indicating the amount of fire the extinguisher will handle. The minimum rating for a Class A extinguisher to be used on minor hazards is 2A. For Class B or C hazards, a rating of 10 is the minimum size recommended. Some have combined ratings.

Extinguishing Agents:

- **Dry Chemical—Standard:** Useful on Class B and C fires (automotive, grease fires, and flammable liquids). Leaves a mildly corrosive residue that can damage electrical equipment.
- **Dry Chemical—Multipurpose:** Useful for Class A, B, and C fires. Effective on most common fires. Highly corrosive with sticky residue. Not for use around electrical appliances or computers.
- **Halogenated Agents:** Useful on Class A, B, and C fires (check labels for specifics). Mildly toxic but versatile, and leaves no residue.
- **Carbon Dioxide:** Useful on Class B and C fires. Very clean with no residue but are heavy, short range and must be applied close to fire.
- **Water-Based Agent:** Use on Class A fires only. These are inexpensive to refill and maintain.

REMEMBER: If an extinguisher is used, you should still call the fire department and evacuate the area. Fire personnel will make sure that the fire is out.

FAMILY RECORDS

Store your important documents and family records—deeds, property records, insurance policies, and other important papers—in a safe place such as a safety-deposit box or in a waterproof and fireproof container at home. Make copies of your important documents for your disaster supply kit. Important documents include:

- ❏ Driver's license and personal identification
- ❏ Passports
- ❏ Birth certificates
- ❏ Social Security cards
- ❏ Deeds and ownership certificates (automobiles, boats, etc.)
- ❏ Insurance policies along with your agent's contact information
- ❏ Wills
- ❏ Current photographs of family members
- ❏ Year, model, license plate number, and identification numbers (VIN) of vehicles
- ❏ Bank and financial account numbers with the appropriate contact information
- ❏ Lease and name and contact information for your landlord or property manager
- ❏ Important medical information (allergies, medications, and medical history)

PERSONAL PROPERTY INVENTORY

Make a record of your personal property for insurance purposes. Take photos or a video of the interior and exterior of your home. Include important personal belongings in your photo inventory.

INSURANCE

If you live in an area that is prone to certain natural hazards—hurricanes, earthquakes, etc.—review your insurance policies and determine what provisions and exemptions may apply to your situation. Household insurance policies generally exclude flood damage from rising water and other specific losses that can occur in the aftermath of a natural disaster. A policy may provide funds to rebuild your home, for example, but not cover the removal of damaged trees from your own property.

If you live in a flood-prone area, consider purchasing flood insurance. Flood insurance that covers the value of a building and its contents will not only provide greater peace of mind but will speed recovery. Be prepared by finding out how you are covered and what you might need to do to secure additional protection.

DIGITAL SURVIVAL—HOME BUSINESS AND COMPUTERS

Home businesses and individuals have come to rely on computers for everything from basic recordkeeping to financial management and tax preparation. Computers, however, are vulnerable to the effects of natural disasters such as power surges or failure and water damage. Data stored on computers can be corrupted or, worse, lost.

By preparing ahead for a potential disaster, you should be able to resume a home business without serious disruption. Take stock of the risks your business might face and make a plan to deal with those risks. Review your plan annually or when changes occur in the business to keep it current.

PROTECT YOUR HARDWARE

- Use a surge protector or an uninterrupted power supply backup to protect data in the event of a power outage. Replace surge protectors at least once a year.
- Keep your computer hardware and software licenses up to date. Maintain hardcopy records such as leases in a secure location.
- Have waterproof tarps to cover computers and equipment in case of water infiltration, and elevate and secure your equipment.

BACK UP YOUR FILES

Protect your vital business and personal records. Back up your data and create a plan to regularly back up your data and protect the backup. Include your key business information—budgets, client lists, sales and tax records, insurance, loans, and banking information. Keep important papers in a safety-deposit box and copies at another safe location.

- Make backups of any business or personal computer files—tax, accounting, production records, inventory, and customer lists.
- Back up your computer data automatically on a daily basis. Check the backup log regularly to ensure that backups are completed

properly. Note that there are online remote backup services available.

- Use a removable or portable data storage device and back up your on-site data to it daily. If you must evacuate, you can easily take it with you.
- Protect your backups by keeping a set of backup files stored off-site and maintain permanent monthly archives. Store these file copies on an off-site server at least 50 miles away from your home or office.

INVENTORIES

- Keep an inventory of all hardware and software with serial, license and model numbers, and company information for leased or purchased hardware and software.
- Keep contact information for the company where you store off-site backups—include contact names and numbers.
- Record the serial and license numbers of all secondary computer devices (printers, hard drives, scanners, etc.).

2. POWER

BLACKOUTS

Power outages can be caused by problems as severe as major faults or failures in a multi-state power grid or regional damage caused by storms, floods, or earthquakes. They can be caused by local damage to neighborhood power lines caused by fallen trees and wind, ice build-up or construction accidents. Some blackouts can be a momentary inconvenience while others can last for a week or more. Whatever the cause, the lights go out.

A power outage can cause the failure of other household systems. Wells and municipal water systems require electrical power to pump water. Forced air and electrical baseboard heating units will not work. Natural gas and oil furnaces require electricity to operate their thermostats, electrical ignition systems, and blowers. Most communications systems will not work without power.

Rolling blackouts occur when a power company shuts down electricity to selected areas to conserve power at times of peak demand—for example, during hot weather when air-conditioning use is at its maximum. These blackouts generally last for about one hour. Hospitals, police and fire stations, and airport control towers are usually exempt. As a rule, rolling blackouts are timed for peak energy usage periods. Power companies will usually announce the schedule for rolling blackouts.

IN THE EVENT OF A BLACKOUT

Turn off or disconnect all appliances, equipment, or electronics that were in use when the power failed. When power is restored, it may come back in a series of surges that can damage computers and the motors in large home appliances (air conditioners, refrigerators, washers, or furnaces). In the event of storm damage, turn off the electricity at the main fuse box or circuit breaker if you can do it safely.

- Leave at least one light turned on so you'll know when the power is restored.
- Use the phone for emergencies only. Never call 911 just to get information.
- Keep the doors of your refrigerator and freezer closed to keep food as fresh as possible.
- If your appliances get wet, first turn off the electricity at the main fuse box or circuit breaker. Then, unplug the appliances and let them dry out. Have an electrician check the appliances before you reconnect them.
- Get some cash for basic expenses in advance. Equipment such as automated teller machines (ATMs) may not work during a power outage.

PREPARING FOR A BLACKOUT
Assemble necessary supplies, including:

- ❏ Flashlights
- ❏ Batteries
- ❏ A portable radio
- ❏ At least one gallon of water per person
- ❏ A small supply of pre-cooked food.

- Have a portable, battery-powered radio. If you have a cordless telephone that requires electricity, plan for alternate communication—a corded phone or cell phone. In a disaster situation, cell phones may not be operable due to damage to local relay centers or usage overload.

- Use a high-quality surge protector on all of your computer equipment. Consider using a battery backup and extra batteries or a power converter that will allow your laptop to be operated from a vehicle cigarette lighter. If you need your computer for a home business, consider installing an auxiliary power supply. In a blackout, some computer network voicemail systems and remote dial-up servers may not operate if the power is out where these systems are located. Even if you have power, your access to remote technology may be disrupted.

- Keep your car fuel tank at least half full because gas stations rely on electricity to power their pumps.

BLACKOUT SAFETY TIPS

- Turn off electrical equipment you were using when the power went out.
- Tune in to local radio or television for the latest emergency updates and news reports.
- Avoid damaged, sparking, or broken wires! Check the electrical system if you can do so safely. If in doubt, leave the building and call for help.
- If you use a generator, connect equipment directly to the outlets on the generator—do not connect the generator to your home electrical system.
- Never run a generator inside a home or garage.
- Use flashlights for emergency lighting. Try to avoid using candles.
- Never burn charcoal for heating or cooking indoors.

IF YOU HAVE A DISABILITY

- If you are on some form of electrical life-support system, make sure you have emergency battery backup.
- If you need medication that requires refrigeration, most can be kept in a closed refrigerator for several hours. Check with your physician or pharmacist.
- If you are deaf or have hearing loss, consider getting a portable battery-operated television set. Emergency broadcasts may give

information in open captioning.
- If you use a motorized wheelchair or scooter, keep an extra battery. You can store a lightweight manual wheelchair for backup.

EMERGENCY LIGHTING
FLASHLIGHTS

Flashlights will be invaluable during any period of time when the electricity is off. The better the flashlight is made, the more reliable it will be.

- **Standard Flashlights:** Regular flashlights come in all sizes with standard or high-intensity bulbs. High-intensity bulbs give off more light but burn out quickly and use more electricity. Make sure you have a good supply of extra batteries and bulbs. Test your flashlight's duration by inserting a new battery and turning it on until the battery is exhausted.
- **Battery-Powered Lanterns:** These larger versions of flashlights are available with bulbs or fluorescent tubes. Regular bulbs provide brighter light but exhaust batteries more quickly than fluorescents.
- **Rechargeable Flashlights:** Most tend to feature heavy-duty construction and in some the rechargeable battery unit is removable for recharging. Outlet rechargeable flashlights tend to hold a short charge.
- **LED Flashlights:** LED bulbs use 10 percent less power than a regular bulb. A flashlight powered by two D-cell batteries should last

for about two weeks. LED bulbs come in blue, yellow, or red. (Red light does not constrict your pupils and permits better night vision.)

- **Alternative Flashlights:** Other flashlight options include wind-up flashlights with a built-in crank-powered battery charger or generator and self-charging flashlights that can be powered by shaking them. Flashlights are also available with a hand-powered, squeeze-type direct generator.

BATTERIES

Keep a supply of batteries on hand. Check what kind you need; most flashlights use D, AA, or AAA batteries. Some lamps use 6-volt batteries. Store batteries in their original containers in a dry storage space at room temperature, away from heat or open flame. *Don't store batteries in the refrigerator.* Batteries stored in the refrigerator generate less power and can form condensation that damages appliances. Properly stored, batteries can last for 3 to 5 years. Remove batteries from battery-powered devices if you plan to store them for more than a month to prevent leakage.

Rechargeable flashlight batteries only work if you are able to recharge the batteries. Rechargeable batteries are effective but wear out more quickly than regular ones. Solar-powered battery chargers are available but require long exposure to sunlight to build up an effective charge. You can also get chargers that draw power from a generator.

GLOW OR LIGHT STICKS

Disposable light sticks are very useful in an emergency and can provide cool, low-level light for several hours. A light stick is composed of a glass vial containing a solution of hydrogen peroxide housed in a larger plastic tube filled with phenyl oxalate ester and a fluorescent dye. When the plastic tube is bent, the glass vial breaks, mixing the two solutions. The resulting chemical reaction causes the fluorescent dye to emit light. There is a minimal amount of toxic material in glow sticks. If a stick breaks and fluid gets into the eye or on the skin, washing with water is the only treatment needed.

OIL LAMPS (KEROSENE) AND CANDLES

WARNING: Candles and oil lamps use an open flame and are significant fire hazards. Use with extreme caution and never within reach of children or pets!

Kerosene Lamps

These lamps burn kerosene or lamp oil through a wick. If you use kerosene, get #1 grade (the product sold as lamp oil is a more refined grade of kerosene). While kerosene or lamp oils give off a lower level of toxic gas, always use them in a well-ventilated area. Never burn gasoline in an oil lamp. If you choose to use kerosene lamps, keep a supply of extra wicks on hand. Kerosene lanterns, generally made with a metal frame and fuel tank, will not break if dropped and are somewhat safer than glass-bodied lamps.

Remember, all kerosene or oil lamps generate a lot of heat, most of which goes straight up the chimney. Keep lamps away from any overhead flammable substance—curtains, electric light shades, wallpaper-covered walls, and low ceilings. Circular-wick and mantel draft-type oil lamps such as Reo and Aladin styles burn very hot and exhaust heat up their chimneys like a blowtorch.

WHITE GAS, GASOLINE, AND PROPANE MANTEL LANTERNS

These liquid-fueled lanterns burn white gas (butane), unleaded gasoline vaporized under pressure and sprayed by a simple carburetor onto a silk mantel for ignition. Propane lanterns use pressurized gas released directly onto the mantel. The fuel burns on the surface of the mantel providing, in most cases, an intense light. Mantels, once ignited, are fragile and require frequent replacement. Liquid-fueled lanterns also require pumping to put the fuel under pressure.

Liquid-Fueled Lanterns

White gas (butane) provides a consistent, intense white light. As with any flammable fuel, however, a spill can be easy to ignite. White gas burns cleanly with little soot and carbon build-up. White gas is easy to find and is sold at most hardware stores as lantern fuel. An average double-mantle white gas lantern puts out more than 60 watts of light and with a full tank will burn for more than an hour and a half at full brightness.

Unleaded gasoline leaves considerable odor and residue and vapors, and accidental spills can ignite explosively. It is not recommended to use unleaded automotive gasoline which contains additives that can clog or gum up lantern carburetors.

Propane Lanterns

These are fueled by screw-in propane canisters. The gas is under pressure and does not require pumping. Propane is clean burning and can put out anywhere from 34 to 235 watts of light. Burn times for an average cylinder can range from about 4.5 hours to 24 hours depending on light output. Propane does not function efficiently at very low temperatures but is more resistant to cold than butane.

WARNING: All of these lanterns give off light by an exposed flame. They should be used only in well-ventilated areas due to fire hazard and risk posed by carbon dioxide or carbon monoxide. Do not attempt to refuel a hot lantern or add fuel indoors!

CANDLES

Candles are easily obtainable and give off a low, but acceptable level of light. They do, however, burn with an open flame and are a primary fire hazard in emergency situations. Hastily mounted in a candleholder or makeshift base, candles can be unstable and easily fall over if left unattended. If you choose to use candles, consider obtaining some kind of candle lantern that will enclose the flame. You can select a candle lantern designed for campers or even a farm lantern. Even when contained in a lantern, however, candles are still a source of fire. Try to avoid using candles, particularly if you have children or pets. If you must use candles, play it safe.

WARNING: Candles pose a significant fire hazard! Always have a fire extinguisher or heavy wool blanket to smother a fire!

GENERATORS

Selecting a Generator

A generator's electrical production capacity is usually rated in kilowatts. Most output ratings are based on the generator's capacity to handle a momentary surge, and the continuous output capacity is usually lower. Electric motors require three to four times the normal current for starting, and combined loads will have considerable startup surge demands.

A generator's rating is also based on output capacity at sea level—the true rating is 3.5 percent less for each additional 1,000 feet of altitude. To choose the proper-size generator, list the total wattage of all appliances and motors that you might want to run at the same time. The total wattage should represent 70 percent of the generator's continuous wattage rating. Appliances and equipment usually have labels indicating their power requirements. For lighting, the light bulb wattage indicates the power needed. If amps and volts are listed, use the following simplified formula:

Amps x Volts = Watts

(Example: 12.5 Amps x 120 Volts = 1,500 Watts)

If the generator does not produce sufficient power for all your needs, plan to stagger the operating times of the devices. Drawing more power than the generator can produce may result in a blown generator fuse or damage to the connected equipment. Make sure the generator is listed with Underwriters' Laboratories (UL).

Generator Types

- **Gasoline:** Gasoline-powered generators tend to be inexpensive but remember, gasoline vapors are explosive and tend to separate and lose octane if stored over a long period of time. A gasoline-powered generator consumes two gallons of gas to produce 10,000 watts of electricity for one hour.

- **Diesel:** Diesel generators may last longer than gas-powered generators but are considerably more expensive. An average diesel-powered generator consumes one gallon of fuel to produce 10,000 watts of electricity for one hour.

  NOTE: In an emergency, you can operate a diesel engine on filtered vegetable oils or an oil/diesel mix. Be aware, however, that such mixtures can eventually damage fuel injectors without special management.

- **Propane:** Propane-powered generators are self-contained and usually intended to provide back-up household power in the event of a power outage. A propane generator uses three gallons of propane to produce 10,000 watts of electricity for one hour.

WARNING: *Propane is heavier than air and quite explosive and should not be used in confined areas.*

GENERATOR SAFETY

The principal safety hazards when using a generator are carbon monoxide poisoning from the exhaust, electric shock, fire, and burns from hot exhaust.

WARNING: *Under no circumstances should portable generators be used indoors or even in partially enclosed areas!*

Opening doors and windows or using fans will not prevent carbon monoxide from building up. Always locate generators outdoors away from windows, doors, and vents. Carbon monoxide is invisible and odorless and can cause unconsciousness and death.

WARNING: *If you feel sick, dizzy, or weak while using a generator, get to fresh air right away.*

To avoid electrocution, always keep the generator dry and operate it on a dry surface under some kind of well-ventilated canopy. Touch the generator with dry hands only. Before refueling, turn the generator off and let it cool down because gasoline spilled on hot engine parts could ignite.

USING A GENERATOR

Plug appliances directly into the generator, using a heavy-duty, outdoor extension cord in good condition that is rated at least equal to the sum of watts or amps of the connected appliance load. The cord should be fitted with a grounded three-pronged plug. Always start the generator before plugging in any cord or appliance.

Never feed power to the household wiring by plugging the generator into a wall outlet. This is called "backfeeding" and is extremely dangerous. Backfeeding bypasses protective devices and can place utility workers at risk of electrocution. If you wish to backfeed into your household system, have a qualified electrician examine the wiring and install a power transfer switch.

It is a good idea to start your generator once a month and let it run for up to 20 minutes. This will prevent gum and carbon buildup that can cause engine malfunction and will ensure that fresh gasoline is added regularly. Use a gasoline stabilizer additive in the fuel tank and keep the metal fuel tanks in older models of generator filled to avoid moisture condensation and resulting corrosion.

Fuel Storage

Always use the type of fuel recommended in the manufacturer's instructions. Store fuel for the generator in an approved safety container outside of living areas. Never store gasoline in your basement or garage because of the danger of vapor ignition. Keep it in a garden shed or ideally in a flameproof

cabinet. Container types include:
- Portable plastic fuel tanks
- 5-gallon jerry cans (steel or plastic)
- 55-gallon steel drums

Fuel Degeneration

There are elements in gasoline that will oxidize. Over time, heat and moisture can cause oxidation that, in turn, causes fuel to develop gum, resin, and varnish, resulting in a reduction in octane. Diesel fuel is more stable than gasoline, but fuel stored for long periods of time collects water from condensation and is vulnerable to microbial infestation. Careful storage solves much of the fuel degradation problem, but even with optimum storage conditions, fuel can degrade without proper fuel treatment. You can reduce the chances of this damage by adding a commercial gasoline or diesel fuel preservative to your fuel stocks. It is best to change the gasoline in your fuel containers at least every three months—empty the cans into an almost full car tank to safely dispose of fuel.

NATURAL GAS SAFETY

Natural gas leaks and explosions cause a significant number of fires following natural disasters. It is a good idea to have everyone in the family learn the proper shut-off procedure for natural gas. Because there are different shut-off procedures for various types of gas meter, contact your local gas company for directions on how to disconnect gas appliances and gas service to your home in an emergency.

If you smell the odor of gas or hear a hissing noise, open a window, shut off the main electrical breaker, and get everyone out quickly. (In the aftermath of a natural disaster, you may notice an overly large consumption of gas being registered on the gas meter.) Turn off the gas, using the outside main valve if you can, and call the gas company from an outside location. Avoid turning on electrical appliances that may cause a spark that can ignite leaking natural gas. Remember, static electricity is also an ignition source—it is very important to get out as quickly as possible and stay out.

Shut off electricity:
- Locate your electricity circuit box.
- Teach all responsible persons in the household how to shut off the electricity to the entire house.
- In the event of power loss, check any pilot lights in gas appliances and make sure that they remain lit. If you cannot relight them yourself, consider shutting off the gas to the appliance.

WARNING: If you turn off the gas for any reason, a qualified professional must turn it back on. NEVER attempt to turn the gas back on yourself.

3. WATER

It seems that during many natural disasters, there is always the problem of having either too much water or not enough. The real problem in most disaster situations, however, is finding water to drink. In the aftermath of disasters such as hurricanes, flooding, or earthquakes, loss of power, contamination, and damage to water delivery and purification systems can disrupt the supply of clean drinking water.

During and after a disaster, water can become contaminated with microorganisms such as bacteria, sewage, agricultural and industrial waste that can cause sickness or even death. Bacteria cause diseases such as dysentery, cholera, typhoid, and hepatitis. Even if you have your own water supply such as a well or cistern, it is possible for power outages, flooding, or other natural disasters to compromise your water source. Wells may be structurally undamaged by flood or earthquake but can be contaminated and should be tested by health officials before use.

While you can get along without food for quite a while, if a disaster occurs, one of the most important things you will need is an adequate supply of clean drinking water. Dehydration is life threatening within two to three days. Having an ample supply of clean water will be a top priority if or when a disaster strikes. An active person needs a minimum of a half-gallon of water to drink each day.

WATER ESSENTIALS

- Keep a three-day supply of water for each family member stored in a cool, dark place, and remember to include additional water for your pets.
- Drink only approved or treated water.
- Never drink floodwater.
- Drink water that you know is not contaminated first. Suspect water from faucets or other sources can be used as long as they have been treated. If treatment is not possible, delay drinking questionable water as long as possible.
- Minimize your water requirements: Hot environments and heavy physical activity can double water requirements—keep cool and reduce physical activity.
- Allow people to drink according to their own needs.
- Try not to ration water unless ordered to do so by the authorities.
- If at all possible, do not substitute carbonated soft drinks for drinking water. Avoid caffeinated drinks and definitely stay away from alcohol; these can cause dehydration and increase your need for drinking water.

BASIC NEEDS

- One gallon per day per person, ½ gallon for drinking and ½ gallon for cooking and sanitation.
- Children, nursing mothers, and sick people may also require additional drinking water.

WATER SOURCES

Bottled Water

Bottled water is the safest and most reliable emergency water supply. If you expect an emergency, purchase commercially bottled water. Keep it in its original container and do not open it until you need to use it. If you plan long-term storage, observe the expiration or "use by" date.

Storing Tap Water

- Purchase food-grade water storage containers from a surplus or camping supplies store.
- Use two-liter plastic soft drink bottles. These make safe and effective water storage containers.
- Avoid plastic milk and juice jugs. The plastic used in these containers prevents you from adequately removing fruit sugars and milk proteins that will provide harmful bacteria with an environment in which they will grow.
- Avoid glass and cardboard containers—glass bottles and containers are heavy and breakable, and cardboard cartons leak and are not designed for long-term storage of liquids.
- Polyethylene (plastic) water containers can be obtained from most food storage or

container companies. Use only high-quality, food-grade containers. If you buy used containers, find out what they previously contained—the taste and odor of the former contents can leach into the plastic over time. Most containers come in 5-, 15-, and 55-gallon sizes. Be aware that when filled with water, a 55-gallon drum will weigh 440 pounds.

Sanitizing and Filling Containers

- Before filling any container with water, thoroughly clean it with dishwashing soap and warm water. Rinse containers completely to be certain that no soap residue remains.

- Sanitize your containers by adding one teaspoon of basic household bleach (nonscented) to a quart of water. Rinse the inside of the container with the solution, making sure that it comes into contact with all surfaces. Pour out the sanitizing solution and thoroughly rinse out the container with clean water.

- Fill the container to the top with tap water. If the water is from a commercially treated water utility and contains chlorine, you do not need to take steps to further sanitize the water. Water from wells and untreated sources (not chlorinated) should be treated with chlorine bleach (see below).

- Use the original cap to tightly close the container. Avoid touching the inside of the cap with your fingers to avoid possible contamination.

- Label the container as drinking water and add the date when it was filled on the outside.
- Store water in a cool, dark place.
- Replace stored water supply every 6 months.

Loss of Water Service

If you suspect that you may lose your water service or if you hear of broken water or sewage lines or are advised by the local authorities of possible contamination, take steps to save a safe supply of drinking water in your home.

- Fill your bathtub and other available containers with water before service is lost.
- Protect the water supply already in your home by shutting off the main water supply. Know the location of the main water line into your home and close the main valve.
- To use the water remaining in your pipes after closing the main valve, you will need to let air into the system from the highest faucet in your home. Open the highest faucet (a small amount of water will trickle out). With this faucet open, you can obtain safe water from the lowest faucet in your home.
- To use water remaining in your hot water heater, turn off the electricity or gas to the tank. Close the cold water intake valve and open the hot water valve; this will permit water to flow out of the bottom drain. Be sure to refill the tank before turning the electricity or gas back on.

Safe Water Sources in Your Home:

- Water remaining in household pipes after the main water line is shut off (before the water supply is contaminated).
- Ice cubes—melt and use.
- Water from the toilet tank (not the bowl). Do not use this water if you have added any chemical treatments (cleaners) to the tank.
- Water in an undamaged hot water heater tank.

Outdoor Water Sources:

WARNING: Assume that all outdoor water sources are unsafe and will require treatment. Particularly avoid water with an unpleasant odor, dark color, or floating debris.

- Consider all wells and cisterns in a disaster area as unsafe to drink until they are tested.
- Water from rainwater, streams, rivers, ponds, lakes, and natural springs should all be treated before drinking.
- Salt water is usable only if distilled into fresh water first. Never drink salt or seawater!

Unsafe Sources:

- Radiators and hot water boiler (home heating system).
- Swimming pools (contain levels of chlorine or other disinfectants too high to drink, can be used for personal hygiene and cleaning).
- Waterbeds may contain fungicides and chemicals leaching from the vinyl which makes the water unsafe for drinking. They are an excellent source of water for flushing toilets.

WATER TREATMENT

All water of uncertain quality should be treated before using it for drinking, food preparation, dishwashing, brushing teeth, or making ice. Treating the water can eliminate harmful organisms and provide you with safe drinking water. There are several ways to treat water and often a combination of treatments is the best solution. Before treating any water, let suspended particles settle to the bottom of the container and strain the water through a coffee filter or clean cloth to remove particles.

Be sure to have the materials necessary to treat water in your disaster kit.

There are three treatment methods:

Boiling—the safest method of treating water.

- Strain water to remove any foreign material.
- Heat water to a rolling boil for at least one full minute; this will kill most organisms. Water boiled at high altitude should be allowed to boil longer—water boils at a lower temperature the higher you go.
- Allow water to cool before drinking.
- You can improve the taste of boiled water by pouring it back and forth between two clean containers; this puts oxygen back into the water.

Chlorination—bleach

- Use regular household liquid bleach containing 5.25 to 6.0 percent sodium hypochlorite.
- Do not use bleach that contains scents or dyes, color-safe bleach or bleach with added cleaners.
- Add 16 drops (1/8 teaspoon) of bleach to

one gallon of water; stir and let stand for 30 minutes.

- Note that this treatment will not kill all parasitic organisms.
- Water should have a slight bleach odor; if it does not, repeat the process and let stand an additional 15 minutes. If, after a second dose, the water still does not have a chlorine smell, discard it and find another water source.

Distillation—using steam

Distillation—boiling the water and collecting the vapor that condenses—will remove germs that resist chlorine as well as heavy metals and salts.

- Fill a pot halfway full with water.
- Tie a cup to the handle of the pot lid so that the cup hangs right side up when the lid is turned upside down.
- Place the lid on the top of the pot upside down; be sure the cup does not touch the water.
- Boil the water for 20 minutes.
- The water that drips from the lid into the cup is distilled.

Other Treatments

- If you use chlorine or iodine tablets, follow the directions on the container. Avoid iodine and chemical treatment products that do not contain 5.25 percent sodium hypochlorite as the only active ingredient.
- Camping water filters vary in level of purification. If you choose to use one, be aware of the level of treatment it offers.

4. FOOD SAFETY

REFRIGERATOR

In the event of a power failure, avoid opening the refrigerator or freezer. An unopened refrigerator will keep foods safe for at least 2 hours. You can insulate the refrigerator somewhat with blankets or quilts—never block the vent. Remember, perishable foods should never be kept at room temperature for more than 2 hours—eat or discard meats, poultry, seafood, dairy products, and all cooked foods if they have been in a closed refrigerator without power (above 40°F) for 4 to 6 hours. Don't rely on odor or appearance of food. Consider keeping a thermometer in your refrigerator; even a short power failure can make food unsafe.

Discard the following food types if kept for more than 2 hours at room temperature:
- Raw or cooked meat, poultry, and seafood
- Casseroles, stews, or soups
- Milk, cream, yogurt, soft cheese
- Cooked pasta, pasta salads
- Fresh eggs, egg substitutes
- Mayonnaise and tartar sauce
- Cream-filled pastries

Foods such as these can be kept at room temperature for a few days:
- Butter, margarine

- Fresh fruits and vegetables
- Opened jars of salad dressing, peanut butter, jelly, relish, mustard, ketchup, olives
- Hard and processed cheeses
- Fruit juices
- Fruit pies, bread, rolls, cakes, and muffins

Discard food that may have come in contact with flood or storm water. Also discard any food in containers with screw-caps, crimped or twist caps, snap-lids, and snap-open tops if they have come in contact with floodwater.

STANDING OR CHEST-TYPE FREEZER

The amount of air space in a chest-type freezer will affect the length of time that food will keep without power. Food in a half-full freezer, where the internal temperature before power failure was at 0°F or below, will keep cold enough for up to 24 hours and in a full freezer for 48 hours.

If you expect a power failure, you can prolong food storage by turning the temperature settings in your refrigerator and freezer to the coldest setting. Fill plastic bags or containers with water, leaving about an inch of space inside each one for expansion as it freezes. Place the containers around food in the refrigerator and freezer. The chilled water or ice will help keep food cold by displacing warm air.

Cooler and Ice

If it looks like the power outage will last for more than 2 to 4 hours, pack perishables into an ice-filled cooler or ice chest. Pack perishables such as meats, fish, poultry, milk, dairy products, eggs, etc. By putting the ice in a plastic trash bag, you can avoid soaking food as the ice melts. Do not leave the freezer lid open for longer than necessary. In a disaster, ice may be distributed by local emergency services.

The greater the surface of your ice pieces, the faster they will melt. For example, crushed and cubed ice will melt more quickly than block ice. A bag of crushed or cubed ice will probably last about 5 to 7 hours in an ice chest, depending on the outside temperature and the quality of the cooler. Block ice is best for keeping your ice chests cold long term. Block ice may be difficult to obtain so, as an alternative, take clean plastic milk bottles and fill them with water and freeze them.

Do not store the cooler in a hot location and keep it out of the sun. Ice will last up to twice as long when the cooler is kept in the shade. Don't rush to drain cold water; recently melted ice keeps food and drinks cold, and melted ice water preserves ice better than empty air space.

Dry Ice

If you have advance warning of a power outage, consider obtaining dry ice for your cooler. Dry ice (frozen carbon dioxide) is particularly useful because of its very cold temperature, -109.3°F. Dry ice will sublimate (evaporate) at a rate of 5 to 10 pounds every 24 hours in a typical ice chest. Dry ice can burn the skin and should be handled with insulated gloves. Dry ice gives more than twice the cooling energy per pound and three times the cooling energy per volume than regular water ice. You can use dry ice to extend the life of regular ice.

POWERLESS COOKING, MEAL PREPARATION, AND FOOD SAFETY

Cook meals using a fireplace (with wood only—no charcoal), camp stove—propane, white gas, alcohol—or outdoor charcoal grill. You can also use a candle or Sterno warmer, such as a fondue pot, chafing dish, or Sterno stove to heat prepared foods. Always make sure to extinguish open flames before leaving the room. Do not use a candle warmer to cook raw meats, fish, and eggs.

WARNING: Never use a fuel-burning camp stove or charcoal grill inside your home, even in a fireplace. Fumes from these stoves can be deadly!

"POWERLESS" FOOD TIPS

- Use perishable foods from the refrigerator and pantry first.
- Use the foods from the freezer second. (Make sure the seal on your freezer door is still in good condition.)
- Use nonperishable foods and staples last.
- Use bottled or boiled water only for food preparation until your water supply is certified safe. Never use water from questionable sources.

- Use canned or powdered milk.
- Use liquids from canned vegetables and fruits for drinking and cooking.
- Select foods that cook quickly, prepare casseroles and one-dish meals, or serve no-cook foods. Packaged survival or camping foods are good choices but require fairly large amounts of water in preparation.
- Avoid salty foods; they will make you thirsty. Instead, eat salt-free crackers, whole-grain cereals, and canned foods with high-liquid content.
- Eat commercially canned foods straight from the can. If you heat it in the can, be sure to open the can and remove the label before heating.
- Do not cook frozen foods because they require much more cooking time and heat than canned goods.
- If you are without refrigeration, open only enough cans or jars for one meal. Don't try to save leftovers.

EMERGENCY FOOD SUPPLY

Choose foods that require no refrigeration and little water, special preparation, or cooking. Familiar foods are important; consider your family's unique needs and tastes. Try to include foods that they will enjoy and that are also high in calories and nutrition.

Remember individuals with special diets and allergies, including babies, toddlers, and the elderly. Canned dietetic foods, soups, and juices may be helpful for elderly people. Make sure you have a manual can opener and disposable utensils. Don't forget nonperishable foods for your pets.

Emergency Foods:

- Ready-to-eat meats, fruits, and vegetables
- Canned or boxed juices, milk, and soup
- High-energy foods such as peanut butter, jelly, low-sodium crackers, granola bars, and trail mix
- Special foods for infants or persons on special diets
- Cookies, hard candy
- Instant coffee
- Cereals
- Powdered milk
- Vitamins and protein supplements

You may not need to go out and buy foods to prepare an emergency food supply. You can use the canned goods, dry mixes, and other staples on your cupboard shelves. Make sure to check the expiration dates and follow a first-in, first-out rule.

STORAGE TIPS

- Keep food in a dry, cool location—a dark area if possible. Place new items at the back of the storage area and older ones in front. Use foods before they go bad, and replace them with fresh supplies.
- Close food boxes and other resealable containers carefully after each use.
- Empty open packages of sugar, dried fruits, etc., into screw-top jars or airtight canisters

for protection from insects and pests. Place perishable foods in plastic bags and keep them in sealed containers.

SHELF LIFE OF FOODS FOR STORAGE
Use Within Six Months:
- Powdered milk—boxed
- Dried fruit
- Dry, crisp crackers
- Potatoes

Use Within One Year:
- Canned condensed meat and vegetable soups
- Canned fruits, fruit juices, and vegetables
- Ready-to-eat and uncooked instant cereals
- Peanut butter
- Jelly
- Hard candy and canned nuts
- Vitamins

May Be Stored Indefinitely (in proper containers and conditions):
- Wheat, soybeans, white rice, dry pasta
- Bouillon products
- Vegetable oils
- Baking powder
- Salt
- Instant coffee, tea, and cocoa
- Powdered milk—in nitrogen-packed cans
- Noncarbonated soft drinks

5. FIRST AID

First aid is the immediate care given to a person who is ill or injured. Identifying a life-threatening condition, protecting the victim from further injury, and fighting the effects of shock are important parts of basic first aid. The goal is not to replace the care of a physician or emergency personnel but to protect the victim until medical assistance arrives. In any life-threatening situation, always call 911 first and get medical help as soon as possible. Intervene only to the extent necessary—don't play doctor!

STOP AND LOOK

Before helping a victim, make sure it is safe to do so. You can't help a victim if you put your own life at risk. Never approach an electrocution victim unless the power is off. If anything dangerous is present, call for help and wait for trained personnel. If the scene is safe, find out what has happened.

PRIMARY VICTIM INSPECTION

Remember, never move a victim unless an immediate life-threatening danger exists, such as fire, flooding, live wires, or the possibility of structural collapse.

Look for the following:

❏ Is the victim conscious?
❏ Is he breathing and does he have an

open and unobstructed airway?

❏ Does he have a heartbeat?

❏ Is he bleeding severely?

REMEMBER: If the victim can talk or cry, he is conscious, breathing, and has a pulse.

If the victim has stopped breathing, call for medical assistance immediately and begin CPR if you are trained to do so.

Seek immediate medical assistance (call 911) if the victim has:

❏ Difficulty breathing

❏ Severe bleeding or is vomiting blood

❏ Unconsciousness or badly confused

❏ Persistent chest pain or pressure

❏ Head, neck, or back injuries

❏ A sudden severe headache and is having seizures, or has slurred speech

❏ Has been poisoned

If Unconscious: Check for ABC: Airway—Breathing—Circulation.

• Place your ear near the victim's mouth to listen and feel for breath. Watch to see if his chest is rising and falling. Check for and clear obstructions.

• Check for a pulse by placing your fingers on his neck, just below the angle of the jaw.

BREATHING

Clear the victim's airway by tilting back his head. Place your palm on the victim's forehead and tilt his head back while grasping and lifting his chin.

Use two fingers to check the victim's mouth for foreign material or obstructions. If the victim still is not breathing, apply mouth-to-mouth resuscitation.

BLEEDING

WARNING: Control serious bleeding immediately!

Arterial Bleeding

Blood from a severed artery is under high pressure and appears bright red and comes in spurts. A cut artery can result in the loss of a large volume of blood in a short time—arterial bleeding must be controlled immediately or death may result.

Venous Bleeding

Blood from a severed vein will appear dark red or bluish in color and will come in a steady flow. Venous bleeding is more easily controlled than arterial bleeding.

Stop the bleeding:

- Apply **Direct Pressure** to the wound. The pressure must be firm enough to stop the blood flow and should be maintained long enough to close the damaged surface.
- Use a **Pressure Dressing.** If bleeding continues after pressure has been applied for about 30 minutes, you should apply a pressure dressing. Use gauze or other material applied directly over the wound and held in place by a tightly wrapped bandage. The bandage should not restrict circulation.

- **Tourniquet.** Use of a tourniquet is not recommended and should be considered only if there is no medical assistance available and the victim has a massive wound with severe, uncontrollable bleeding.

SHOCK

Shock is the body's reaction to a serious injury, illness, or other traumatic event. It is a life-threatening condition that occurs when the victim's physical and mental functions are seriously impaired by lack of oxygenated blood reaching the lungs, heart, or brain. The more severe the injury, the more likely the victim is to suffer shock. Shock can be deadly if not treated quickly.

Look for these signs of shock:

- ❑ Anxiety
- ❑ Weakness
- ❑ Paleness
- ❑ Sweating
- ❑ Thirst
- ❑ Rapid but weak pulse
- ❑ Dizziness and fainting

Treating Shock

- A conscious victim should sit or lie on a blanket on the floor, so that he will be safe if he loses consciousness. Place an unconscious victim on his stomach with his head to one side (as long as no neck injury is suspected).
- Except in the case of a head wound, lower

his head and shoulders and raise his feet approximately 15 inches.
- Keep the victim warm, and protect him from cold. Remember to insulate him from the ground.
- Reassure the victim.

WOUNDS

Major open wound:
- Cover the wound with a clean cloth or sterile pad and press firmly.
- Elevate the wound above the heart.
- Secure the sterile pad with a roll bandage to hold it in place.
- If bleeding does not stop, add additional bandages over the roll.
- Seek medical help as soon as possible.
- Do not remove an embedded object— apply pressure around it.

Minor open wound:
- Stop the bleeding by applying direct pressure with a clean cloth or bandage; if one is not available, use your fingers.
- Once blood has soaked through the bandage, place another on top. Do not remove the first bandage, as removal will disturb the clotting that has already taken place.
- If the bleeding continues, elevate the wound higher than the heart.
- Once the bleeding stops, clean the wound gently to remove dirt and debris.

- Apply antibiotic ointment if available.
- Wrap the wound with a cloth bandage; be sure that you do not cut off the circulation.

FRACTURES

Relocating or setting bones can be difficult and should not be attempted as further, more severe injury may result. Call 911 and wait for help. A simple fracture can be treated by immobilizing the injured limb with an improvised splint to reduce pain and prevent further injury.

FIRST-AID KIT

You should have a first-aid kit to keep in your disaster supplies kit as well as one for each car. First-aid kits approved by the American Red Cross are available for purchase, or you can assemble your own kits. Always remember to keep adequate supplies of prescription medicines and other special needs for the elderly, infants, and people with serious allergies. *(See Basic First-Aid Kit, page 146.)*

6. HEAT AND COLD

HEAT

If the weather is exceptionally hot, take steps to remain cool. Avoid strenuous activity; if you must do strenuous work, work during the coolest part of the day—usually in the early morning hours. Stay indoors as much as possible. Move to the lowest level of your home, since cool air falls. If you go out, wear lightweight, light-colored clothing and a hat.

Drink plenty of water, even if you don't feel thirsty. Water is the safest liquid to drink during heat emergencies—avoid drinks containing alcohol (including beer) or caffeine, since these beverages dehydrate the body. Avoid using salt tablets unless directed to do so by a physician. Sport drinks are particularly effective in preventing dehydration. Remember to provide plenty of fresh water for your pets.

During excessively hot weather, eat small meals and eat more often. Avoid foods that are high in protein; these increase metabolic heat.

While heat can affect anyone, it is more likely to affect young children, elderly people, and people with health problems. For example, persons with poor blood circulation and those who take diuretic medications may be more susceptible. Discuss these concerns with a physician. If the heat is intense and the power may be off for some time, consider going to a "cooling shelter" that may be opened in your community.

HEAT EMERGENCY SYMPTOMS

Heat Exhaustion

Heat exhaustion occurs when people exert themselves in a hot environment where body fluids are lost through heavy sweating. The body increases blood flow to the skin, decreasing blood flow to vital organs, resulting in a form of mild shock. If not treated, the victim may suffer heat stroke. Symptoms include cool, moist, pale, or flushed skin; heavy sweating; headache; nausea or vomiting; dizziness; confusion; and exhaustion. The body temperature will be near normal.

Emergency Treatment

Get the person out of the heat. Loosen tight clothing and apply cool, wet cloths to the body. If the person is conscious, give them a half glass of cool water to drink every 15 minutes. Make sure they drink slowly. Allow the person to rest in a comfortable position, and watch carefully for changes in condition.

For Heatstroke or Sunstroke

The systems that control sweating cease to function and core body temperature can rise so high that brain damage and death may result. The body must be cooled quickly. Symptoms include hot, red skin; rapid, weak pulse; quick, shallow breathing;

and changes in consciousness. Body temperature can be extremely high—as high as 105°F. Generally, the skin will feel dry.

WARNING: Heatstroke is a life-threatening situation!

Get help, if possible, by calling 911 or your local emergency number. Move the person to a cooler place. Quickly cool the body by immersing the victim in cool water, or wrap wet sheets around the body and fan it. Watch for breathing problems. Keep the person still, and cool the body any way you can. Do not give the victim anything to drink if they are unconscious, semiconscious, or vomiting. *NOTE: Take an American Red Cross first-aid course to learn how to deal with heat emergencies.*

COLD

During severe winter storms, your home heating system could be out of action for several days. Elderly people are the primary victims of hypothermia. Many older persons freeze to death in their own homes after being exposed to dangerously cold indoor temperatures. A number of persons, even younger people, are asphyxiated by carbon monoxide due to improper use of fuels such as charcoal briquettes indoors. In addition, house fires occur more frequently in the winter due to lack of proper safety precautions when using alternative heating sources. If the power may be out for a prolonged period, consider going to another location that has heat (the home of a relative, friend, or a public facility). Think about your neighbors—you may be able to stay warmer together. You can also contact your local emergency management authorities for information on public shelters.

Reduce discomfort:
- Stay indoors where it is warmer.
- Conserve body heat by putting on extra layers of clothing. Wearing layers of loose-fitting, lightweight, warm clothing will keep you warmer than a single, bulky garment. However, be prepared to remove layers of clothing to avoid overheating, perspiration, and subsequent chill.
- Your bed may be the warmest place in the house. Add extra blankets to trap body heat. This is a good way to keep children warm.
- Huddle together to conserve body heat. Several people staying together in one room will help everyone stay warm.
- Eat regularly to provide the body with the energy it needs to produce its own heat.
- Drink plenty of fluids to prevent dehydration. Avoid caffeine and alcohol, stimulants which cause dehydration and accelerate the symptoms of hypothermia.

EMERGENCY HEATING

In a severe cold situation, select a room to be heated. (See Winter Storms, page 99.) Close off all rooms except the one you plan to heat. If you are using a vented stove or space heater, select a room with some sort of stove or chimney flue. If possible, choose a room on the warmest side of the house, away from prevailing winds. Confine emergency heat to a small area—don't choose large rooms or rooms with large windows or uninsulated walls. Keep doors closed.

WARNING: Think safety first in a heating emergency!

Space Heaters

Your chances of freezing to death in your home are pretty small, but fire, asphyxiation from carbon monoxide and other combustion pollutants, or lack of oxygen are very real dangers unless you take proper safety precautions. Any type of nonelectric heater should always be thoroughly vented. Have a professional connect the vent or stovepipe to a chimney flue or other adequate vent. Never run emergency vents close to flammable materials such as wooden window sashes, curtains, and shades. Also, remember that flues suitable for low-temperature gas-burning appliances may not be safe to vent hotter oil, coal, or wood smoke. Always have at least one person stay awake to act as "firewatcher" and keep some kind of fire-fighting equipment handy.

If you have to use an unvented gas or kerosene heater, provide for plenty of ventilation in the room. Whenever the heater is in use, cross-ventilate by cracking a window an inch or so on either side of the room.

Emergency Heating Equipment

(See Winter Storms, page 99.)

- A fireplace with ample supply of wood.
- A small, well-vented wood, coal, or tent stove with fuel.
- A portable space heater or kerosene heater. Check with your local fire department for local regulations concerning the use of kerosene heaters. Keep portable heaters at least three feet away from furniture and other flammable objects, and ventilate the room.
- Gas-fired hot water heater. (Your gas-fired heater may not function if you have an electronic thermostat.)

Common fuels include: firewood, coal, kerosene, gasoline, wood chips, camp stove fuel, alcohol, tightly rolled newspapers, and magazines.

You can burn coal in a fireplace or stove if you make a grate to hold it, allowing air to circulate underneath. Metal screening placed on wood grate will keep coal from falling through.

UNVENTED GAS OR KEROSENE HEATERS

WARNING: Unvented kerosene heaters are illegal in many states—unvented heaters can pose a serious threat of asphyxiation!

If you absolutely have to use an unvented gas or kerosene space heater, take special precautions:

- Buy only space heaters that are certified to meet current safety standards by organizations such as the Underwriters' Laboratories and the American Gas Association Laboratories.

- Use only space heaters manufactured after 1982. These will have an oxygen depletion sensor that shuts off the heater if there is insufficient fresh air or the heater is beginning to produce excess amounts of carbon monoxide.
- Gas heaters should have a pilot safety valve that shuts down the gas should the pilot light go out.
- Have a heating professional inspect your space heater at the beginning of every heating season.
- Burn only water-free, "clear white," 1-K kerosene in kerosene heaters. Never use gasoline, fuel oil, diesel, or yellow (regular) kerosene.
- Never sleep in any room with an unvented gas or kerosene heater.
- Keep heater away from curtains, drapes, bedding, furniture, or other flammable material.
- Always refuel the heater outside with the unit turned off. Never refuel inside or while heater is in operation. When refueling, do not fill the heater's fuel tank completely since cold kerosene expands as it warms.

WARNING: Any nonelectric alternative heat source (fireplace, wood stove, or space heater) can be dangerous—observe fire safety rules, keep an approved fire extinguisher on hand and ventilate the room properly. Do not store fuels near the stove, fireplace, or heating device, especially if you use highly combustible materials such as gasoline or kerosene. Never use your gas oven as a source of heat, and never burn fuels such as charcoal briquettes inside— even in a fireplace!

PROTECT YOUR HOME

- Make sure your house is properly insulated. Caulk and weather-strip doors and window-sills to keep out cold air.
- Cover windows with plastic from the inside.
- Protect exposed plumbing if it seems likely that your heat will be off for several hours in below freezing temperatures. Know how to shut off water valves. Drain pipes (including hot water heating pipes) in any rooms where temperature falls below 40°F. Drain pipes such as those in the sink, tub and shower traps, toilet tanks and bowls, hot water heater, and furnace boiler.

7. COMMUNICATIONS

The chances are excellent that some or all of the communications systems you depend upon for normal everyday use will break down as a result of a natural disaster. Regular telephone landlines are easily severed, and power failure can affect many communications systems. A cell phone can be a valuable asset in an emergency situation, but it may or may not function, depending on the situation.

INFORMATION
Radio and TV Broadcasts
Your best source for information during a disaster will be provided by local radio or television stations or over the Emergency Broadcasting System. If the power fails, you should have a battery-powered radio or TV and extra batteries.

COMMUNICATIONS PLAN
When a disaster strikes your family may be separated by school, work, or errands. Make a plan for how you will contact each other. Make sure that every family member has a complete list of contact numbers and select a friend or relative who lives out of state for family members to notify that they are safe. A copy of your list of contact numbers should be included in your disaster supply kit.

NOAA Weather Radio

NOAA Weather Radio (NWR) is the best means for receiving warnings from the National Weather Service. The National Weather Service continuously broadcasts updated weather warnings and forecasts that can be received by special NOAA Weather Radios. NOAA Weather Radio is an all-hazards radio network broadcasting warnings and information for all types of hazards, both natural and technological. NOAA radios are available with a Specific Area Message Encoder feature, which automatically alerts you when a watch or warning is issued for your county.

TELEPHONES

- Make a list of important telephone numbers (doctor, work, school, and relatives) and keep it in a prominent place near the phone in your home.
- Post emergency telephone numbers by all phones (list fire, police, etc.).
- Choose an out-of-area family contact.
- Make sure all family members memorize this person's name and telephone number, and know they should call your family contact if they get separated from the family.

After a Disaster

Use the phone only if it's absolutely necessary as emergency crews will need all available phone lines. It is often easier to call out of the region, as the local phone lines might be tied up.

Landlines

Landlines (communications that require strung or buried wires) will continue to function (as long as they are intact) even during a power failure, since they are powered through the phone lines. Portable telephones will not work without electricity; have at least one corded phone in your home. Pay phones will often work when home lines are out.

Cell Phones

During an emergency, cell phone systems can become overloaded with the volume of call traffic. In addition, power outages can affect local servers, and severe storms can destroy or disable transmission towers. Conserve battery life by turning off your cell when not in use. You can recharge your cell phone by using a car charger or other cell phone accessory chargers. Solar and hand-cranking chargers are available.

Satellite Phones

Satellite phones work in emergencies by transmitting calls through networks of low-earth-orbiting satellites. They generally will not work indoors and are heavy and more expensive than cell phones. Satellite phones are available for purchase or rent through several sources.

RADIOS

CB Radios

Citizens Band (CB) refers not to a type of radio, but to the regulations regarding their use. CB sets may be of use in an emergency when other methods of communications are down. CB equipment is relatively inexpensive and can be a good alternative to a cell phone or landline.

Walkie-Talkies

Walkie-talkies are hand-held two-way radios with a limited range of anywhere from ½ mile to five miles. Walkie-talkies can be effective tools for short-distance communications and will be used by emergency and rescue personnel for local communication.

HAM Radio

Amateur radio, or HAM radio, refers to a set of rules and regulations and not to a type of radio equipment—you must be licensed to be a HAM radio operator. HAM radio operators can provide local and long-distance communications (via shortwave broadcasts) during regional, national, and international emergencies when other means of communications are out. HAM operators usually coordinate with government and private relief services.

8. EVACUATION

There are some situations where it is just too dangerous to try and ride out a natural disaster at home. State authorities often call upon residents of the Gulf Coast and Atlantic seaboard to evacuate their homes and businesses in the face of powerful hurricanes. In addition, transportation and industrial accidents can result in the release of harmful chemicals, forcing the evacuation of entire neighborhoods. Wildfires, particularly in the western states, and flooding frequently cause hasty evacuations.

When such disasters strike, emergency management officials will provide evacuation information to the public via local radio and television broadcasts and by using the National Emergency Broadcasting System. If local officials ask you to evacuate, do so immediately. Depending on the situation, the amount of time you have to evacuate will vary. A hurricane may allow several days to prepare for an evacuation, while other situations, such as a hazardous material spill or chemical release, may allow only moments to get away.

Advanced planning will make any evacuation easier. Contact your local emergency management office to learn about the possible dangers in your area ahead of time, and find out about emergency warning systems along with evacuation routes and plans. Consider assembling a family disaster supply kit and make an evacuation plan. Remember, an evacuation can last for several days or longer and during that time you may be responsible for part or all of your own food, clothing, and other supplies.

PREPARE FOR EVACUATION

- Find out about evacuation plans for your community.
- Prepare a disaster supply kit. *(See Disaster Supply Kits, page 142.)*
- Discuss possible evacuation procedures with your family and make sure that everyone knows what to do.
- Plan a destination outside the potential disaster area in advance and get a map of the area.
- Locate the public emergency shelters in your region.
- Establish a check-in contact—a friend or relative outside your area—so that everyone in the family can call in to report that he is safe. Make sure all family members have that phone number.
- Find out where children will be sent if they are evacuated from their school.
- Keep a full tank of gas in your car if an evacuation seems likely. Gasoline may be unobtainable during a major evacuation.
- If you do not own a car or other vehicle, make arrangements for transportation with a

friend, or contact your local emergency management office. Public transportation systems may not be available during an emergency.

- Make plans for pets and other domestic animals.
- Know how to shut off electricity, gas, and water at the main switches and valves. Make sure you have the tools you need (usually pipe and crescent or adjustable wrenches). Contact your local utility providers for additional information.

EVACUATION SUPPLIES

Assemble any supplies that you might need if you were to be away from home for several days and place them in an easy-to-carry container. Label the container clearly and keep it in a designated, easily accessible place. Remember to include all of the disaster supply kit basics. You might consider assembling a car kit to keep in your vehicle that contains emergency supplies in case you are stranded; include flares, jumper cables, and seasonal supplies in addition to your disaster supply kit. *(See Disaster Supply Kits, page 148.)*

If ordered to evacuate:
- Listen to a battery-powered radio for evacuation instructions.
- Take your disaster supply kit with you if you are ordered to evacuate.
- Wear sturdy shoes and clothing that will provide some protection, such as long

pants, long-sleeved shirts, and a cap or hat.
- Follow the recommended evacuation routes.
- Stay away from downed power lines.
- In a flooding situation, watch out for washed-out roads and bridges. Never try to drive through flooded roadways or bridges—find another way around.

If you have time:
- Let others know where you plan to go and leave a note telling when you left and your destination.
- Close and lock doors and windows.
- Unplug electrical appliances—radios, televisions, freezers, refrigerators, toasters, and microwaves.
- Make arrangements for pets.
- Shut off water, gas, and electricity and secure propane tanks before leaving, if instructed to do so.

If you have to leave immediately, take:
- Medical supplies: prescriptions and other necessary medications.
- Disaster supplies: flashlight, batteries, radio, first-aid kit, bottled water.
- Clothing and bedding: a change of clothing and a sleeping bag or bedroll for each member of the household.

PAPERS AND DOCUMENTS

You may want to consider consolidating important records and storing them in a safe, portable container. Make sure that your container is waterproof—a file box, plastic tub or box, or even sealable plastic freezer bags. If lost, these records may be difficult and time-consuming to replace.

- Driver's license, passport, or other personal identification
- Social Security cards
- A supply of cash
- Checkbook and credit cards (credit card and bank account information)
- Birth and marriage certificates
- Immunization records
- Proof of residence (deed or lease)
- Insurance policies (home, renters, auto, life, etc.)
- Wills and contracts
- Copies of recent tax returns

RETURNING HOME AFTER THE DISASTER

- Monitor radio and television broadcasts for information and instructions.
- Telephone your family and friends as soon as possible to tell them you are safe.
- Do not return until the local authorities confirm that it is safe.
- Do not reenter the house until authorities tell you it is safe to do so.
- Use caution when entering buildings that may have been damaged or weakened.
- Use a battery-operated flashlight or glow

stick for light. Do not use exposed flame light sources in damaged buildings. There is a danger of flammable materials and leaking gas.

- If you suspect a gas leak or if you smell gas, leave the house immediately and notify the gas company or the fire department. Do not turn on the lights; a spark from the switch might ignite the gas.
- Notify the power company or fire department if you see damaged electrical wires.
- If any of your appliances are wet, turn off the main electrical power switch before attempting to unplug them. Dry all appliances, wall switches, and sockets thoroughly before you reconnect them.
- Check all food supplies for spoilage or contamination.
- Do not drink local water until it has been certified safe.
- Wear sturdy shoes or boots and use heavy gloves when handling debris.
- Watch for venomous snakes in flooded structures and debris.

9. DISASTERS

HURRICANES

Hurricanes are tropical cyclones, huge low-pressure systems that form in the South Atlantic and gain in intensity as they move westward into warmer offshore waters. In the Northern Hemisphere, hurricanes are characterized by a counterclockwise movement of winds and are generally accompanied by thunderstorms and heavy rain. All Atlantic, Caribbean, and Gulf of Mexico coastal areas are subject to hurricanes or tropical storms. The Atlantic hurricane season lasts from June to November, with the peak season lasting from the middle of August to late October. Parts of the southwestern United States and the Pacific coast can also be affected by heavy rains and flooding caused by hurricanes spawned off the Mexican coast.

Hurricanes begin as tropical depressions, organized systems of clouds and thunderstorms with a distinct surface circulation and maximum sustained winds of 38 mph or less. When upgraded to a tropical storm, it will be characterized by a system of strong thunderstorms with a defined surface circulation and maximum sustained winds of 39 to 73 mph. The storm becomes a hurricane when it develops into an intense tropical weather system of strong thunderstorms with an organized surface circulation and maximum sustained winds of 74 mph or higher.

Hurricanes can cause catastrophic damage to coastlines and for several hundred miles inland as well. Winds in the most severe hurricanes can exceed 155 miles per hour, and hurricanes and tropical storms can create deadly and destructive storm surges (massive domes of water pushed onshore by high winds) along low-lying coastal areas and cause extensive damage from heavy rainfall. Storm surges can reach as high as 25 feet and can be 50 to100 miles wide. Hurricanes may also spawn tornadoes.

While hurricanes are most threatening to populations living along coastlines, these devastating storms can also travel inland for hundreds of miles, causing damage through heavy rains, flooding, and tornadoes. When slow-moving tropical storms move into mountainous areas, they tend to produce heavy rain, triggering flooding of river and stream basins and flash flooding.

Hurricanes are classified into five categories based on wind speed, central pressure, and damage potential.

CATEGORY	SUSTAINED WIND (mph)	DAMAGE	STORM SURGE
CATEGORY 1 Agnes (1972) Irene (1999) Gaston (2004)	74 to 95	**MINIMAL:** Unanchored mobile homes, vegetation, and signs	4 to 5 feet
CATEGORY 2 Frances (1985) Floyd (1999) Bob (2004) Irene (2005)	96 to 110	**MODERATE:** All mobile homes, roofs, small craft; flooding	6 to 8 feet
CATEGORY 3 New England (1938) Gloria (1985) Fran (1996) Ivan (2004)	111 to 130	**EXTENSIVE:** Small buildings; low-lying roads cut off	9 to 12 feet
CATEGORY 4 Hazel (1954) Hugo (1989) Charley (2004) Dennis (2005)	131 to 155	**EXTREME:** Roofs destroyed, trees down, roads cut off, mobile homes destroyed, beach homes flooded	13 to 18 feet
CATEGORY 5 "Labor Day" (1935) Camille (1969) Andrew (1992) Katrina (2005) Wilma (2005)	More than 155	**CATASTROPHIC:** Most buildings destroyed, vegetation destroyed, major roads cut off, homes flooded	Greater than 18 feet

STORM INFORMATION:
HURRICANE WATCH AND WARNING

In the event of an approaching storm, government authorities will issue one of the following warnings:

- *Hurricane or Tropical Storm Watch:* A warning that hurricane or tropical storm conditions are possible in a specified area, generally within 36 hours.
- *Hurricane or Tropical Storm Warning:* Hurricane or tropical storm conditions are expected in a specified area, usually within 24 hours.

Storm status will be broadcast on local radio and TV stations and by NOAA Weather Radio. NOAA Weather Radio, a public service of the National Oceanic and Atmospheric Administration, is a nationwide network of radio transmitters that broadcast continuous weather information 24 hours a day. NWR requires a special radio receiver or scanner to receive the signal.

Prepare for a hurricane:

- When a hurricane WATCH or WARNING is issued for your area, listen to NOAA Weather Radio or local radio or TV stations for current storm information.
- Contact your local emergency management or planning and zoning office to find out if you live in an area that is prone to flooding during a hurricane.
- Bring in all trash cans, lawn furniture, and anything else that can be picked up by the wind.
- Clean clogged gutters and downspouts.

- Clear branches from trees and shrubs near your home that might be torn loose by high winds.
- Prepare to cover all your windows. Permanently installed storm shutters offer the best protection for windows. If you do not have storm shutters, have cut-to-fit $\frac{1}{2}$- to $\frac{5}{8}$-inch marine (outdoor) plywood sheets ready so that you can quickly install them to cover windows. Predrill holes in the plywood and install wall anchors so that you can put them up quickly.
  Note: Tape (masking or duct) does not prevent windows from breaking; taping windows is not an effective substitute for shutters or plywood.
- Prepare for power failure. *(See Power, page 19.)* Be prepared to turn off electricity, gas, and water if authorities advise you to do so. You should have written directions on hand to help recall shut-down procedures.
- If you own a boat, find out how and where to secure it.

EVACUATION

Listen to emergency broadcasts on local radio and TV stations or NOAA Weather Radio for evacuation instructions. If advised to evacuate, do so immediately! If an evacuation route is suggested, plan to use it. Local authorities will probably announce the establishment of shelters in public buildings.

Know when to evacuate:

- If you are directed to do so by local authorities.

Be sure to follow their instructions.
- If you live on the coast, on a floodplain, near a river, or on an inland waterway.
- If you live in a mobile home. Trailers or mobile homes are particularly dangerous during high winds and flooding, no matter how well fastened to their foundation.

SAVE YOUR LIFE! Don't wait until the last minute to leave by making last-minute preparations in hopes of saving your possessions; know when to cut and run!

Evacuation Plan: Decide ahead of time where you could go. Prepare an evacuation kit. *(See Car Kit, page 148.)* Select several places—a motel, designated shelter, or even a friend's home away from the danger zone. It's a good idea to share your plan with relatives or friends. Keep a list of telephone numbers of the places you plan to go along with a road map of your locality in your evacuation kit. You may find that you need to take alternate routes if major roads are closed or clogged. If you have limited time to prepare for evacuation, take only necessary medicines, blankets, a flashlight, and a battery-powered radio with you. Don't take chances; getting safely away from the storm area should be your first consideration. *(See Evacuation, page 67.)*

If you stay at home during a hurricane:
- Stay indoors and away from windows. Keep curtains and blinds closed. Despite the temptation to watch the storm, stay in the center of your home, away from windows.

- **Safe Room:** Establish a safe room in your home. If you live in a one-story house, the strongest room is often a closet or bathroom near the center of the house, away from exterior doors and windows. In a two-story house, the strongest space is often a closet near a stairwell on the ground floor. If you live in a high-rise building, consult with your building management to select a safe area. Your safe room should be able to hold all of your household members at one time. Stock your safe room with emergency supplies. *(See Disaster Supply Kits, page 141.)* Bring ice and some drinks in a thermos or cooler. (It can get really hot in your shelter.) If you plan to bring a pet, you will need a pet carrier. Discuss possible exit routes from your home, and what to do if someone smells gas or smoke.
- Know about storm conditions. If you are in an area where the eye of the storm will pass, be aware that the calm that happens is deceptive. The worst part of the storm will come after the eye passes and the winds blow from the opposite direction. Trees, buildings, and objects that have been damaged by the first winds can be broken or destroyed by the following gusts. Watch for tornadoes which may occur both during and after a hurricane. *(See Tornadoes, page 113.)*
- Have a supply of clean drinking water on hand. *(See Water, page 34.)*

AFTER THE STORM

- If you are evacuated, return home only when local officials tell you it is safe to do so.
- Avoid floodwaters. If you encounter a flooded road, turn your car around and go another way. Moving water is very heavy and can wash your car away; as little as 6 inches of water can stop your engine or cause you to lose control of your vehicle. Two feet of water carry away most cars. If you are caught in rapidly rising floodwaters, get out of the car and move quickly to higher ground.
- Some family members may not be at home when a storm strikes; agree on a place to meet after the storm. In the aftermath of a storm, it may be easier to make long-distance calls rather than local ones. Make sure that everyone knows the telephone numbers of one or two out-of-town relatives who can be contacted in an emergency.
- Inspect your home for damage.
- Keep copies of your insurance policies in a waterproof container (a zip-lock plastic bag will do) with you in your safe place. *(See Family Records, page 15.)* You might be forced to leave your home immediately after the storm.
- Remember to bring your wallet and your house and car keys with you if you take shelter in the safe room.

FLOODS AND
FLASH FLOODS

Floods are among the most common natural hazards in North America and are responsible for millions of dollars in property damage annually. Floods can range from local events that affect a single community to widespread events covering entire river basins over several states. Flooding can follow in the aftermath of hurricanes, severe thunderstorms, prolonged rain, the breakup of an ice jam or dam, along with levee and flood wall failure. Flooding along rivers can occur seasonally following winter snowmelts and spring rains. Water rapidly fills rivers and overflows the banks onto normally dry land. Overspill from rivers or streams will usually increase slowly. Hurricanes and tropical storms can produce coastal flooding—the result of storm surge and heavy rains. Severe coastal flooding can also be produced by tidal waves (tsunamis)—the result of marine volcanic activity or earthquakes.

A flash flood is the fastest-moving type of flood and can generate walls of water that reach heights of more than 15 feet. Generally, flash floods are the result of heavy rainfall—slow-moving thunderstorms or heavy rain from tropical storms—that falls in a concentrated area. These floodwaters move at very fast speed, carrying rocks, trees, mud and other debris. Flash floods develop quickly, often in just a few minutes and occasionally without any visible signs of rain. Even small streams, drainage channels, canyons, gullies, and culverts can flood suddenly, catching people off guard and creating very dangerous situations. In desert areas, arroyos, water-carved ravines, and dry creek beds are particularly subject to flash floods. Runoff from far-off storms can quickly fill dry watercourses, transforming an empty basin into a fast-moving river. If it has been raining hard for several hours, or raining steadily for several days, be alert to the possibility of a flash flood.

Be aware of the dangers of flooding no matter where you live, but especially if you live in a low-lying ground, along a river or watercourse, or downstream from a dam. Contact local land-use authorities for information about flood risk in your neighborhood. While most people living away from low-lying areas will never have to face rising water flooding, anyone can encounter flash floods when traveling in their vehicle. If you come upon flash flood conditions, play it safe; turn around and go another way!

PREPARE FOR A FLOOD

- Find out if your home is located in an area where flash floods are likely by contacting the county geologist or your county planning department.
- Learn about community emergency plans, evacuation routes, and the location of emergency shelters.
- Consider raising your furnace, water heater,

and electric panel if they are in a part of your home that may be flooded. You can also consider installing sump pumps with backup power.

- Install "check valves" in sewer traps to prevent floodwater from backing up into the drains.
- A more elaborate preparation is to construct barriers (levees, flood walls, berms, and drains) that will stop or deflect moving water around your home. Seal basement walls with waterproofing compound to block seepage.
- Anchor outdoor fuel tanks. An unanchored tank can be swept away and damage other property.

Insurance: Check your homeowner's insurance policy to find out if flood damage is covered. You will find that flood losses are usually not covered under most homeowner's policies. If you are not covered, consider obtaining a separate flood insurance policy.

- The Federal Emergency Management Agency (FEMA) manages the National Flood Insurance Program, offering federally backed flood insurance to selected floodplain communities.
- Private flood insurance coverage is also available in most communities. Be aware, however, that there is usually a 30-day waiting period before flood insurance goes into effect. *(See Insurance, page 151.)*
- Keep current copies of insurance policies and all important papers or valuables in a safety-deposit box.

FLOOD AND FLASH FLOOD ALERTS

Listen to local radio or TV stations or NOAA Weather Radio for flood information. They will issue a flood or flash flood watch or warning. If directed to evacuate, do so as soon as possible. Watch for signs of flash flooding and be ready to evacuate fast!

- *Flood Watch:* A flood is possible in your area.
- *Flood Warning:* Flooding is already occurring or will occur soon in your area.
- *Flash Flood Watch:* Flash flooding is possible in your area.
- *Flash Flood Warning:* A flash flood is occurring or will occur very soon.

PREPARATION AND EVACUATION

If you have time:

- Secure your home. Move your furniture and valuables to the upper floors of your home and bring in outdoor furniture or tie it down securely.
- Locate your disaster supply kit. *(See Disaster Supply Kits, page 141.)*
- Have your immunization records handy, particularly your last tetanus shot.
- Turn off utilities at the main switches or valves if instructed to do so. Unplug electrical appliances.

REMEMBER: Don't touch electrical equipment if you are wet or standing in water and don't wade in water where electrical appliances are plugged in!

• Make sure you have a full tank of gas in your car in the event that you have to evacuate.

If a flash flood warning is issued, or if a flood warning indicates rapidly rising waters, evacuate immediately. Don't wait for instructions to leave. You may have only moments to escape. Move quickly on foot to high ground away from watercourses—rivers, streams, and storm drains.

WARNING: Be safe! Head for high ground and stay away from the water!

FLOOD SAFETY TIPS

• If forecasters predict storms, stay away from streams, ditches, and gullies.
• Never try to outrun a flash flood down a canyon, arroyo, or flood control channel.
• *Driving:* If you come across a flooded road in your car, turn around and go another way. Moving water is heavy and can easily wash your car away—as little 6 inches of water can cause you to lose control of most passenger vehicles and 2 feet of water can wash away even a pickup or SUV. If your car is caught in rapidly rising floodwaters, get out of the car fast, if possible, and move quickly to higher ground. If the water is coming up fast, don't try to wade to dry ground. Remember, 6 inches of moving water can knock you down. Climb to the roof of your vehicle and call for help.
• *On foot:* Don't wade through moving water.

If you absolutely have to cross a flooded area, walk where the water is not moving. Use a stick to check the ground in front of you. **REMEMBER: Crossing moving water is dangerous. Don't get carried away!**

- If someone is swept away in floodwaters, don't try to go in after them. If possible, throw the victim a detached flotation device (car seat or large, closed ice chest).
- Never tie a rope around your waist to enter fast-flowing water or toss someone a rope to try and pull them out. It will be nearly impossible for even the strongest person to pull you to safety. The force of the water can trap you beneath the surface.

AFTER A FLOOD

- **Drive with caution:** Avoid moving water and watch for areas where floodwaters may have weakened road surfaces.
- **Be careful:** Downed power lines and damaged underground lines pose a serious danger of electrocution. Stay away from floodwaters in areas with fallen or sparking power lines. Report damaged lines to the power company as soon as possible.
- Listen to local radio for news and announcements for the flooded area. Return home only when authorities announce that it is safe.
- Find out whether the local water supply is safe to drink.

- Avoid floodwaters; they are likely to be contaminated with a mixture of oil, gasoline, or sewage. While skin contact with floodwater does not necessarily pose a serious health risk, keep any open cuts or sores as clean as possible to prevent infection.
- Avoid eating any foods that may have been contaminated by floodwater.
- Do not allow children to play in flooded areas. Wash their hands often and do not allow them to play with potentially contaminated toys. You can disinfect most plastic and metal toys by washing them in a solution of one cup of bleach to five gallons of water.

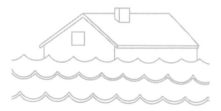

EARTHQUAKES

Severe earthquakes are among the world's most frightening and destructive natural disasters. An earthquake is the sudden movement of part of the earth's crust caused by the sudden slip of a fault. The rock slips suddenly, releasing energy in waves that travel through the earth's crust to cause earthquake tremors. Most earthquake-prone faults occur in the zones between the earth's tectonic plates. The plates, which normally move freely against each other, occasionally become locked together and are unable to release their accumulated energy. Pressure builds and when the plates break free, the sudden violent movement creates an earthquake. Fault slippage expands along the fault line during the quake and can extend for hundreds of miles.

In the event of an earthquake, you first will usually feel a swaying or small jerking motion, then a slight pause, followed by a more powerful rolling or jerking motion. The extent of the movement depends on the earthquake's magnitude, distance from the epicenter, and the geology of the ground. During minor earthquakes, the shaking usually lasts only a few seconds. Violent movement from a major earthquake usually lasts less than one minute.

Most serious earthquakes in the United States in recent years have occurred along the major fault lines in California, such as the 650-mile-long San Andreas Fault, but there are fault zones in other regions that have the potential to cause earthquakes. Historically, the New Madrid seismic zone, located in the central Mississippi Valley (Arkansas, Missouri, Tennessee, southern Illinois, and Kentucky), has been the scene of significant earthquakes in the past. States with the most recorded earthquakes above 3.5 include Alaska, California, Hawaii, Nevada, Washington, Idaho, Wyoming, Montana, Utah, and Oregon. If you live near a quake-prone fault zone, you should learn what to do if the earth moves.

EARTHQUAKE TERMS

- *Epicenter:* The area on the earth's surface directly above the point on the fault where the earthquake began.
- *Seismic Waves:* Vibrations in the earth that travel rapidly outward from the quake's epicenter. The earth movement caused by the seismic waves causes most of the damage during earthquakes.
- *Magnitude:* The amount of energy released during an earthquake.
- *Intensity:* The amount of shaking created by the earthquake and its effects at a particular location on people, structures, and land.
- *Aftershock:* An earthquake of similar or lesser intensity that follows the main earthquake.
- *Richter Scale:* A mathematical formula used to compare the size of earthquakes. The magnitude of an earthquake is based on the maximum extent of seismic waves recorded

by seismographs. While the Richter scale has no upper limits, rock mechanics seem to rule out earthquakes smaller than −1 or larger than about 9.5.

Richter Scale	Effects
3.5 and under	Recorded on scientific instruments but usually not felt.
3.5–5.4	Generally felt, but rarely causes damage.
Under 6.0	Felt over small regions. Can cause slight damage to well-constructed buildings and major damage to poorly constructed ones.
6.1–6.9	Can be destructive in areas up to about 50-60 miles across.
7.0–7.9	Major earthquake. Can cause serious damage over larger areas.
8 or greater	Great earthquake. Can cause serious damage in areas several hundred miles across.

PREPARE FOR AN EARTHQUAKE

If you live in an earthquake-prone area:

Practice Drills: Plan and practice what to do in the event of an earthquake. By planning and thinking ahead, you can be ready to react properly if a quake happens. An important thing to remember is that most deaths and injuries that happen during earthquakes are caused by rubble from collapsing structures and heavy falling objects. Know where to go and what to do if you feel the earth shift. During an earthquake, you have to react quickly. Identify the safe areas in your home—under a sturdy table or against an inside wall away from heavy items that might fall on you. Consider holding family earthquake drills to make sure that everyone knows how to react and where to go in order to protect themselves.

Prepare your home:

- Have a professional check the foundation of your house and determine how the structure is anchored to it. Make sure the sill plate of the house is securely bolted to the foundation. You may be able to take steps to have it strengthened; there are a variety of products called holddowns available for securing walls to the foundation.

- Brace your chimney; it may come down during an earthquake, in particular the freestanding section above the roof line. Secure it to the framing of the roof with sheet metal straps and angle bracing.

- Inspect and repair any defective electrical wiring. Most gas and water lines are rigid and can be torn from their connection points during an earthquake; consider having flexible utility connections installed. Unless you really know what you are doing, it is important to get professional help. Don't try to work on gas or electrical lines yourself.

- Secure your water heater (a ruptured gas line is a major fire hazard), refrigerator, furnace, and any other heavy appliances to wall studs with heavy-duty strapping or, in the case of the water heater, use metal plumbers' tape.

- Fuel oil and propane tanks can shift during an earthquake, breaking the supply line and causing a fire. Tanks should be securely anchored to the floor; consider having a qualified, licensed contractor install flexible hose connections. (Propane tanks are usually property of the propane company; contact them before making any modification.)
- Store large or heavy objects on lower shelves in your house, and keep breakables on lower shelves or in cupboards that fasten shut.
- Reinforce the attachments of overhead lighting fixtures and ceiling fans and make sure that shelves, mirrors, and large picture frames are securely attached to the walls.
- The normal exits from your home or office may become damaged or blocked. Plan for an alternate exit from each room and acquire any special equipment that you may need such as rope or metal ladder.

DURING AN EARTHQUAKE

Indoors:

- Get quickly to the nearest shelter in the room.
- Take cover under a sturdy desk or table or take cover against an inside wall. These can protect you from falling debris and provide an air space if the building collapses. Hold on to your shelter and protect your eyes by pressing your face against your arm. Stay

there until the shaking stops. If you are in bed when an earthquake strikes, stay there. Hang on and protect your head with a pillow.

- If you can't get under a solid item of furniture, crouch in an inside corner and protect your head with your arms. You can also take shelter under the frame of a well-supported doorway. Inner walls or doorframes are the least likely to collapse during an earthquake. Find out which doorways in your home, school, or office have load-bearing frames.
- Avoid taking shelter near windows, outside doors or walls that could shatter or collapse. Stay away from anything that could fall on you like lighting fixtures or heavy furniture or appliances.
- Stay inside until the shaking stops. Be certain that everything has stopped before you try to enter or exit from any building. Debris may continue to fall and lights may be out and hallways and stairwells may be blocked by ceiling tiles, lighting fixtures and other debris.

WARNING: Never use elevators!

- If you are in a crowded place, don't try to rush for the doors, you might get caught in a crush of people. Move away from display shelves and take cover; remember to shield your head.

Outdoors:

- Stay where you are until the shaking stops. Crouch and protect your head with your arms.
- Move away from buildings and power lines. Don't try to run into a nearby building for

shelter. Many earthquake injuries are caused by falling structural elements near doorways and walls.

- If you are in a moving vehicle, stop as quickly and safely as possible and pull over to the shoulder or curb. Keep away from utility poles, overhead wires, trees, and roadway overpasses. Stay in the vehicle and set the parking brake. Remain in the vehicle until the shaking stops.
- If you become trapped under rubble in a building:
  - Never light a match or lighter; there is danger of fire and gas.
  - Keep still; avoid kicking up and breathing toxic dust.
  - Cover your mouth with clothing or a handkerchief.
  - Signal for help by tapping on a pipe or wall that will transmit sound to rescuers.

AFTER AN EARTHQUAKE

In the aftermath of an earthquake, the affected area might suffer fires, building collapse, chemical spills, landslides, dam breaks, and tidal waves.

- Be prepared for aftershocks. These additional shock waves are generally less intense than the main earthquake and may be severe enough to cause damage to already weak-ened structures.
- Listen to a battery-powered radio—the

power may be out—for emergency information in the aftermath of a quake.

- Stay away from downed power lines, or anything in contact with downed lines. Report any electrical hazards to the emergency authorities.
- Use extreme caution around damaged structures. It's a good idea to avoid them if you can.
- If you live along the coast, be aware of the possibility of tidal waves (seismic sea waves), also called tsunamis. If local authorities issue a tsunami warning, stay away from the beach!

In your home:

An earthquake can damage gas, electrical and water lines. Follow all safety precautions if you detect or suspect damaged gas and electrical lines. *(See Power, page 19.)*

- Shut off the water supply at the main valve if water pipes are damaged.
- Open cabinets cautiously. Beware of objects that can fall off shelves.
- Clean up any spilled flammable liquids or other hazardous materials.
- Check your sewage lines for damage before using bathrooms or plumbing.
- Plan to have your house checked for structural damage by a structural engineer.

Evacuation Plans

In the aftermath of an earthquake, you may need to evacuate a damaged area. Be prepared to respond quickly and efficiently to directions from civil authorities. *(See Evacuation, page 67.)*

LANDSLIDES AND MUD SLIDES

A landslide happens when gravity overcomes the stability of masses of earth, rock, or debris on a slope. This can occur when heavy rains, rapid snowmelt, construction of buildings and roads, alternate freezing or thawing, earthquake and even volcanic eruptions change the soil conditions on a slope or hillside. Mud slides are landslides that develop when water rapidly accumulates, softening the ground on a slope, resulting in a fast-moving flow of water-saturated earth. Mud slides tend to follow the path of gullies or drainage channels. Mud slides usually accelerate to about 10 miles per hour, but can move at speeds in excess of 35 miles per hour. The consistency of the flow ranges from watery mud to thick, rocky mud carrying boulders and trees. Slopes disturbed by forest and brush fires or human activity are particularly vulnerable to landslides during and after heavy rains.

WARNING SIGNS

- Look for patterns of water drainage on slopes, and check hillsides for signs of land movement—small landslides or debris flows or progressively tilting trees.
- Find out whether landslides can occur in your area by contacting local geological surveys or departments of natural resources.
- Talk to your insurance agent. Debris flow may

be covered by flood insurance policies from the National Flood Insurance Program (NFIP).

- Assume that steep slopes and areas burned by wildfires are vulnerable to landslides and debris flows.
- Watch the patterns of storm-water drainage on slopes, especially the places where runoff water converges. Watching for small changes could alert you to the potential of a greater landslide threat.

IF YOU LIVE IN AN AREA VULNERABLE TO LANDSLIDES

- Monitor radio or TV broadcasts for warnings about heavy rainfall.
- Watch for an increase or decrease in water level on a stream or creek; this might indi-cate a debris flow upstream. The color of the water flow in a creek or stream may change from clear to muddy water.
- A trickle of flowing mud may precede a larger flow.
- Look for tilted trees, fences, and for fresh erosion or bare patches on slopes.
- Listen for any unusual noise that might indicate moving earth.
- During severe storms, consider leaving; if you choose to stay, move to a second story if possible.

IF YOU SUSPECT IMMINENT LANDSLIDE DANGER

- Be prepared to move quickly; save yourself, not your possessions! Moving debris can flow quickly and sometimes without warning.

DURING A LANDSLIDE

- Get out of the path of a debris flow. Move quickly away from the path of the slide to the nearest high ground away from the path of the flow.
- If escape is impossible, curl into a tight ball and protect your head.

AFTER A LANDSLIDE

- Stay away from the slide area. There may be danger of additional slides.
- Search for injured and trapped persons without entering the direct slide area and be prepared to direct emergency responders to their location.
- Report broken power lines to the appropriate authorities.

WINTER STORMS

Winter storms can range in intensity from moderate snowfall that lasts for a few hours to blizzards that paralyze whole regions for several days. Severe winter storms are distinguished by very low temperatures, high winds, and heavy, blowing snow. The heavy snowfall and extreme cold can immobilize entire regions, shutting down cities and trapping motorists in their cars and can be accompanied by flooding, storm surge, blocked roads, and downed power lines.

Winter storms can also bring sleet (rain that freezes into ice pellets before reaching the ground) and freezing rain (rain that freezes as it falls on surfaces that are at temperatures below freezing). Freezing rain can form a glaze of ice on trees, cars, roads and other surfaces. Ice storms break down trees, disrupt communications and power, and make driving and walking extremely hazardous.

The leading causes of death or injury during winter storms are from automobile accidents followed by exhaustion and heart attacks caused by overexertion. Many elderly people literally "freeze to death" in their own homes after being exposed to dangerously cold indoor temperatures. Others, including able-bodied individuals, are asphyxiated by improper use of combustible fuels like kerosene and charcoal briquettes. In addition, house fires occur more often due to carelessness in the use of alternative heating sources.

WINTER STORM AND BLIZZARD WATCH AND WARNING

- **Winter Storm Watch:** A winter storm is possible in your area.
- **Winter Storm Warning:** A winter storm is occurring, or will soon occur, in your area.
- **Blizzard Warning:** A storm with sustained winds with gusts up to 35 miles per hour, accompanied by heavy snowfall, with visibility less than a quarter mile, is expected to continue for three hours or longer.
- **Heavy Snow Warning:** Issued when 4 or more inches are expected during a 12-hour period, or when 6 inches or more are expected during a 24-hour period.
- **Frost or Freeze Warning:** Below-freezing temperatures are expected.
- **Traveler's Advisory:** Falling or drifting snow, strong winds, freezing rain, or sleet will make driving hazardous.
- **Wind Chill:** An effect that combines the cooling effect of wind and cold temperatures on exposed skin. Wind carries heat away from a person's body at an accelerated rate, driving down the body temperature.

WARNING: Remain alert!

- Listen to local radio or television stations or NOAA Weather Radio for updated information. Remember to keep a battery-powered radio on hand along with fresh batteries.
- Watch the weather. Be aware of changing

local weather conditions.

- Move pets or domestic animals to a sheltered area. Make sure that there is a water supply; most animal deaths in winter storms are caused by dehydration.
- Avoid unnecessary travel.

PREPARE FOR A WINTER STORM AND COLD WEATHER

Emergency Supplies

Stock up on emergency supplies in the event of a power failure—food, water, heating supplies, etc.—in case a storm hits. It's a good idea to have at least a week's worth of food and water supplies. *(See Water, page 34, and Food Safety, page 42.)*

To prepare for extreme cold, add the following to your disaster supply list:

- A warm coat, hat, and gloves or mittens for each member of the family
- Rock salt (or melting compound) to melt ice on walkways
- Sand or non-clumping cat litter to improve traction
- Snow shovels and other snow removal gear
- Extra blankets and bedding
- Safe emergency heating and lighting equipment *(See Power, page 19.)*

Winterize your home:

- Before winter, check your roof for broken, damaged, or loose shingles and small holes. Examine the flashing around all dormers, vent pipes, and chimneys.

- Check weather stripping around windows and doors. Make repairs as necessary.
- Install storm windows or tape clear plastic to the inside window frame.
- Consider insulating the walls and attic; adequate insulation will reduce heat loss.
- Check batteries in smoke and carbon monoxide alarms.
- Clean leaves, dirt, and debris from gutters and downspouts.
- Have a qualified serviceman clean and check your furnace and flues.
- Clean or install new furnace filters.
- Prepare snow removal gear.

Prevent ice dams on eaves:

Ice dams (ice that forms when water from snow melts on a poorly insulated roof and refreezes along the eave line) prevent water from draining and can cause considerable damage to the roof and inside walls of a house.

- Insulate between the top-floor ceiling and the attic, or along the underside of the eaves, if the attic is used as living space.
- Ventilate the attic through windows and louvers when insulation is added to the attic floor. This will help reduce moisture condensation in the attic.

Prevent frozen water pipes:

- Wrap water pipes in insulation or layers of newspaper. Cover newspaper with plastic

to repel moisture.
- Let faucets drip slightly to avoid freezing.
- Drain water from swimming pool and water sprinkler supply lines.
- Remove and drain outdoor hoses. Close the inside valves supplying outdoor hose faucets. And open the outside valves to drain water. Keep the valve open so that any water remaining in the pipe can expand without breaking the pipe.

Insurance

Melting ice and snow can cause flooding in flood-prone areas. Consider purchasing flood insurance to cover possible water damage that may occur during a thaw. Homeowner's policies usually do not cover damage from rising water, so ask your insurance agent about the National Flood Insurance Program if you may be at risk.

Winterize your car:

- Keep the gas tank full for emergency use and to keep the fuel line from freezing.
- Make sure the battery and ignition system are in good working order; clean the battery terminals.
- Check antifreeze levels. Make sure they are sufficient to avoid freezing. Also ensure that the thermostat works properly.
- Check the condition of the heater, defroster, and windshield wipers. Add washer fluid.
- Make sure the exhaust system is in good shape; carbon monoxide is deadly and

usually gives no warning.

- Check your oil for level and weight. Remember, heavier oils congeal more at low temperatures.
- Consider purchasing all-weather radials, snow tires or chains. Make sure the tires have adequate tread.
- Keep a windshield scraper and small broom in your car to remove ice and snow.
- Assemble a car emergency kit. *(See Disaster Supply Kits, page 148.)*

CONSERVE HEAT DURING A WINTER STORM OR A BLIZZARD

Select a room to heat in the event of a power failure. *(See Power, page 19.)* Close off all rooms except the one you plan to heat. Confine emergency heat to a small area; don't choose large rooms or rooms with large windows. Keep doors closed and consider hanging blankets or drapes over doorways to help retain heat.

If you are using a vented stove or space heater, select a room with some sort of stove or chimney flue. If possible, choose a room on the warmest side of the house, away from prevailing winds.

If you have power:

- Conserve fuel. Winter storms can place great demand on electric, gas and other fuel distribution systems. Suppliers may have difficulties in making deliveries or replenishing depleted supplies. Lower the thermostat to 65°F during the day and 55°F at night.

- Close draperies at night. Regular draperies reduce heat loss slightly; insulated draperies are even more effective.
- Seal openings that allow cold air leakage from the attic, and stuff towels in cracks under doors.
- Close fireplace dampers when not in use to keep warm air from escaping up the chimney.
- Think about your neighbors; helping an elderly or infirm person before a storm may be safer and more effective than waiting until after the storm has hit. Encourage them to stay with you or with a friend or relative rather than alone.

Take care of yourself:

- Stay indoors and dress warmly. Wearing layers of loose-fitting, lightweight, warm clothing will keep you warmer than one bulky garment. Remove layers to avoid overheating, perspiration and chill.
- Eat regularly. Food provides the body with energy it needs to produce heat.
- Drink plenty of fluids to prevent dehydration. Avoid caffeine and alcohol. Caffeine is a stimulant and accelerates the symptoms of hypothermia. Alcohol is a depressant that slows circulation and accelerates the effect of cold on the body.

BE AWARE: Babies and the elderly are more at risk from the cold.

If you must go outside: Wear layered clothing, mittens or gloves, and a hat. Your outer garments should be tightly woven and water repellent. A hat or cap will prevent loss of body heat; more than half of your body heat loss is from the head. Mittens are generally warmer than gloves because they contain a larger air space and fingers maintain more warmth when they touch each other.

- Cover your mouth and nose with breathable fabric to protect your lungs.
- Keep dry; wet clothing loses much of its insulating value. Change wet clothing frequently to prevent chill and loss of body heat.
- Be careful to avoid overexertion, such as shoveling heavy snow or pushing a stalled car. The strain from the cold and exertion may cause a heart attack. Sweating can lead to a chill and hypothermia.
- Walk carefully on snow-covered or icy sidewalks. Slips and falls are among the most common causes of injury in winter storms.

MEDICAL EMERGENCIES: HYPOTHERMIA AND FROSTBITE

BE AWARE: In any severe medical emergency, get professional emergency help if possible.

Hypothermia is caused by abnormally low body temperature—less than 95°F. Symptoms include uncontrollable shivering, slow speech, lapse of memory, loss of balance, drowsiness, and exhaustion. Hypothermia is easily treatable but can be life threatening and has the potential to cause organ damage.

* **Emergency Treatment:** Begin warming the person slowly and seek immediate medical assistance. Warm the person's trunk first, using your own body heat, if necessary. Be gentle; rough handling can induce heart failure in severe cases. Warm arms and legs last to avoid forcing chilled blood toward the heart; this, too, can result in heart failure. Remove wet clothing and wrap the victim's entire body in a blanket—a sleeping bag, tarp or plastic bags will work. If the victim is conscious, give them warm foods and plenty of fluids containing sugar. Never give a hypothermia victim alcohol or caffeine.

Frostbite is freezing of the skin and tissue that results from a severe reaction to cold and windy weather conditions. Frostbite can cause permanent tissue damage. Symptoms include a loss of feeling, and the skin (most commonly of the fingers, toes, nose, or earlobes) appears white and waxy. The affected area may feel hard, like a piece of wood.

* **Emergency Treatment:** Seek emergency medical assistance, if possible. Get the victim into a warm environment and rewarm the affected area in tepid water as quickly as possible to reduce the likelihood of permanent tissue damage. Use water heated to 104°F and circulate the water to keep the affected part in contact with the warmest water, avoid rubbing the frostbitten area. This process can last for 30 to 45 minutes and can be quite painful. The frostbitten part is thawed when the skin returns to a pink or reddish color. If blisters occur in the affected area, apply antiseptic ointment and cover with a loose sterile dressing.

Plumbing System: If your power and heat are off for several hours or more during below-freezing temperatures, you will need to keep exposed heating pipes from freezing. Water expands as it freezes and can break pipes, particularly those that are exposed to severe cold such as lines to outdoor hose faucets and water supply pipes in unheated interior areas. You may not become aware of the problem until the water thaws and you have a flood to deal with!

- Circulate water through the pipes. Moving water does not freeze easily. Allow cold water to drip from your faucets.
- If the room temperature drops to below 40°F, however, you may want to consider draining the pipes. Familiarize yourself with your system and consult with an expert and learn what you need to do ahead of time.
- Shut off the water at the main valve or turn off the well pump. Drain the pressure tank, if there is one, and open all faucets until they drain completely. You can drain the system by disconnecting a pipe joint close to the main valve. Drain or put antifreeze in unused toilet bowls.
- Thaw frozen pipes. After the freeze, locate the suspected frozen area, remove any

insulation and completely open all faucets. Keep faucets open; running water through the pipe will help melt ice. Pour hot water over the pipes, starting where they were most exposed to cold air. Apply heat until full water pressure is restored. Do not use a blowtorch or other open flame device. Water in a frozen pipe may boil and cause the pipe to explode.

WINTER DRIVING

Traveling during severe winter weather can be extremely hazardous. If you must drive, consider the following:

- Drive only if it is absolutely necessary.
- Plan trips carefully. Listen for travel warnings on the radio or call the state highway patrol for the latest road conditions.
- Stay on main roads and plan to travel during daylight.
- Travel with someone else if at all possible and check your car for emergency supplies before you leave.
- Let someone know your destination, route, and when you expect to arrive. Ask them to notify help if you are very late.
- If you have a cell phone or two-way radio, keep the battery charged and keep it with you when traveling in winter weather.
- Pack a car emergency kit. *(See Disaster Supply Kits, page 148.)*

- Avoid icy roads if possible. Remember, sleet, freezing rain, freezing drizzle, and dense fog can make driving very hazardous and bridges freeze before roadways.
- Take warm clothes and a good jacket and hat.

If you are trapped in your car by a blizzard or winter storm:

- Pull off the highway. Turn on your hazard lights and display a brightly colored cloth (preferably red) as a distress flag on the radio antenna or in a window. You can also raise the hood after snow stops falling.
- Stay calm. Remain with your vehicle where you are sheltered and rescuers are most likely to find you. Don't leave the vehicle unless help or shelter is nearby. You can easily become disoriented in poor visibility and blowing snow.
- Open a downwind window for ventilation. Freezing wet and wind-driven snow can seal the passenger compartment and suffocate you. Keep warm by turning on the engine and heater for about 10 minutes each hour. Even with a clear exhaust pipe, carbon monoxide can build up inside a standing vehicle while the engine is running. Running the heater for 10-minute cycles will reduce the risk of carbon monoxide poisoning and conserve fuel. Periodically clear snow from the exhaust.
- Leave the overhead light on when the engine is running so that work crews or rescuers

can see you. Take care to avoid running down the car battery.

- Insulate yourself from the cold. Wrap your body and head with extra clothes, blankets, newspapers, maps, or removable car mats. Layering items will help trap more body heat. Huddle together for warmth.
- Try not to stay in one position for too long. Do light exercises to maintain body heat; clap hands and move arms and legs occasionally.
- Watch for signs of hypothermia. One of the signs of hypothermia is sleepiness. If you're alone, stay awake as much as possible. If you have a companion, take turns sleeping; don't allow everyone in the car to sleep at the same time. If you don't wake up periodically to increase body temperature and circulation, you can freeze to death.
- Drink fluids to avoid dehydration. Dehydrated individuals are more susceptible to the effects of cold. Avoid eating snow; it lowers the body temperature.
- If you become stranded in a remote area, tramp "HELP" or "SOS" in an open area in the snow. Stomp large block letters deep enough to create a strong shadow. This should be visible to rescue personnel searching the area by aircraft. Engine oil can be burned in a hubcap to create a smoke signal. To light, prime the oil with a little gasoline or use paper as a starter.

AFTER A WINTER STORM

- Keep listening to local radio or TV newscasts or NOAA Weather Radio for updated information and instructions.
- Listen to the forecasts and be prepared when venturing outside. Major winter storms are often followed by even colder conditions.
- Roads may be blocked and access may be limited to some parts of the community.
- Help any neighbor who might require special assistance, particularly elderly people and those with disabilities.

TORNADOES

A tornado is a violent whirlwind formed when a warm, humid air mass collides with a cold front. Tornadoes take the shape of a vortex—a dark funnel-shaped rotating cloud—that extends from a cloud to the ground and is usually accompanied by intense thunderstorms. The rotating winds within a tornado can reach speeds of 300 miles per hour, causing a destructive updraft within the funnel. Tornadoes generally occur near the trailing edge of a thunderstorm and can also occur during tropical storms or hurricanes. Most tornadoes occur east of the Rocky Mountains during the spring and summer months. Peak tornado season in the southern states is March through May and in the northern states during late spring to early summer.

Tornadoes strike quickly, with little or no warning. These violent storms change direction without warning, demolishing neighborhoods and randomly destroying houses, public buildings, and power lines. They are capable of uprooting trees and flinging large objects, such as trucks and automobiles, over considerable distances. The average forward speed of a tornado is around 30 mph, but can be as fast as 70 mph. The damage path of a tornado can be in excess of 9 miles long by 200 yards wide.

Tornado funnels can be nearly transparent or appear simply as a cloud of rotating debris until they develop clouds or pick up dust. Most tornadoes are clearly visible, but rain or low-hanging clouds can conceal others. Tornadoes that occur over lakes and oceans are called waterspouts. Waterspouts generally do not affect heavily populated areas and are less destructive due to a slower rotation. They can, however, move inland to become tornadoes.

TORNADO WATCH AND WARNING

Tornado Watch: Tornadoes may occur. Be ready to seek shelter immediately if conditions get worse.

Tornado Warning: A tornado has been sighted or indicated by weather radar. Take shelter immediately.

Severe Thunderstorm Watch: Severe thunderstorms may happen in your area.

Severe Thunderstorm Warning: Severe thunderstorms are occurring in your area.

WARNING: Remain alert!

- Listen to radio or television newscasts or NOAA Weather Radio for current information on changing weather conditions. Remember to keep a battery-powered radio on hand along with fresh batteries.
- Pay attention to approaching storms; tornadoes often accompany thunderstorms. Monitor changing weather conditions during a severe thunderstorm watch or warning.

SIGNS OF A TORNADO

A large, black approaching funnel cloud is a pretty sure sign of trouble, but be aware that some tornadoes can strike without much warning. You can't always depend on seeing that funnel since clouds or rain may block your view. The following weather signs may indicate that a tornado is approaching:

- Dark sky with greenish light.
- Large, dark, low-lying clouds.
- Winds die down and the air may become very still.
- Loud roar—like an approaching train.

If you spot a tornado that does not pose an immediate danger to you, report it to the local emergency authorities (call the regular number—save 911 for life-threatening emergencies) or contact your local radio or TV station.

WARNING: If you see approaching storms or any of the danger signs, take shelter immediately!

Local Tornado Warning Systems: Most tornado-prone areas have a siren tornado warning system. Learn the difference between the siren warning signals for a tornado watch and a tornado warning.

SHELTER

There is no completely safe place during a tornado but by knowing where to take shelter, the risk of injury can be reduced. Remember that flying debris causes most injuries and deaths during tornadoes and get under some kind of cover quickly!

House or apartment:

- Avoid windows. Exploding glass can injure or kill.
- Move to the interior part of the basement or an inside room, without windows, on the lowest floor—a central hallway, bathroom, or closet. Stay away from corners, doors, windows, and outside walls.
- Take shelter under something sturdy such as a heavy table or workbench. If possible, cover yourself with a blanket, or mattress, and protect your head with anything available.
- Be aware whether there are heavy objects above your refuge—pianos, refrigerators, book shelving—these may fall through the floor in the event of a tornado strike.

Mobile home:

WARNING: Never stay in a mobile home during a tornado!

Mobile homes, even those with tie-down systems, cannot withstand tornado winds and pressure. Mobile homes can turn over during strong winds.

- Go immediately to a tornado shelter if one has been constructed in your community.
- Go to a nearby building, preferably one with a basement.
- Get out of your mobile home; lie flat in the nearest ditch, ravine, or culvert (see "Outdoors," page 117).

In a vehicle:

The worst place to be during a tornado is in a car

or truck. Motor vehicles are easily overturned or tossed by tornado winds.

- Stop your vehicle and get out; you may not be able to outrun a tornado, particularly in a congested urban area.
- Never take shelter under your vehicle.
- Take shelter in a nearby ditch or depression *(see "Outdoors" below)*.
- Do not take shelter under an overpass or bridge. You are safer in a low, flat location.

Outdoors:

- Lie down flat on the ground in a ditch or low spot.
- Protect your head with some kind of cover, or shield your head with your hands and arms.
- Avoid areas with trees.
- Stay away from vehicles.

Offices, schools, hospitals, churches, or other public buildings:

- Stay away from windows and glass doors.
- Locate a predesignated shelter if possible.
- Move to an interior space on the lowest possible floor.
- Avoid elevators. Power failure can leave you trapped.

Shopping mall, theater, or gym:

These buildings often have long-span roofs supported only by the outside walls. These can collapse if struck by the enormous pressures generated by a tornado.

- Stay away from windows and glass doors

and move to the lowest level of the building.
• Get under a doorframe or huddle against
  a structure that will deflect falling debris—
  heavy counters, supporting walls, under
  theater seats.

PREPARE FOR A TORNADO

Safe Room: If you live in a region where tornadoes are frequent, consider constructing a safe
room in your home. Safe rooms (storm cellars)
built below ground level provide the greatest protection but other locations can be effective. Locate
your safe room in the basement; on a concrete
slab-on-grade foundation (a foundation formed
from a mold set into the ground); a garage floor;
or an interior room on the ground or first floor.
  • Anchor the safe room to resist overturning
    and uplift.
  • Walls, ceilings, doors, and all connections
    must resist high winds and be strong
    enough to stop windborne objects.
  • Underground safe rooms must not flood
    during heavy rains.

Reducing Household Hazards

While no amount of preparation will eliminate
every risk:
  • Bolt walls securely to the foundation.
  • Attach wall studs to the roof rafters with
    metal hurricane clips.
  • Secure large appliances, especially water heat-
    ers, with flexible cable or metal strapping.

WILDFIRES

Dry weather, overgrown forest, brush, and grasslands combined with lightning, human carelessness and arson are all prime ingredients for wildfires. While wildfire is part of the natural system, out-of-control forest and brush fires destroy thousands of acres of timber and property annually. There are three different classes of wildfire. The most common is a surface fire where a slow-moving fire burns along the forest, killing or damaging trees. Ground fires, usually started by lightning, burn on the forest floor or in the ground litter. Crown fires are spread rapidly by the wind and move quickly, jumping along the tops of trees. Danger zones include all wooded, brush, and grassy areas. A major wildfire will leave acres of scorched and barren land in its wake. Wildfires often begin unnoticed and spread quickly, igniting brush, trees, and nearby buildings.

Most forest fires are started by human activity—arson, negligent handling of cigarettes and matches, or improperly extinguished campfires. The other chief cause of forest fires is lightning.

Keep a firesafe home:

If you live in a wildfire-prone area:

- Find out about local evacuation procedures.
- Contact your local fire department or forestry office for information about fire regulations and any wildfire risk in your neighborhood. Fire officials can provide specific information about fire-resistant

construction techniques and materials along with information on wildfire mitigation.

- Create a 30- to 100-foot safety zone around your home. Remove leaves, dead limbs and twigs and clear any flammable vegetation. Remove dead branches that extend over the roof and clean dead leaves and debris from beneath porches and buildings. Prune tree branches and shrubs within 15 feet of a stove-pipe or chimney. Clear a 10-foot area around propane tanks and the barbecue. Stack fire-wood at least 100 feet away from your home.
- Keep roof surfaces and gutters clean and free of combustible debris.
- Mow grass regularly; tall, dry grass is highly flammable.
- Inspect your chimney at least twice a year and keep it clean. Consider installing spark arresters.
- Install smoke detectors on every level of your home, particularly near sleeping areas.
- Make sure you own basic fire tools—a rake, ax, handsaw, bucket, and shovel. Obtain a ladder that will reach the roof.
- Purchase a garden hose that is long enough to reach all areas of your house and any other structures. Remember, you will need an adequate outside water source. You may want to consider purchasing a gasoline-powered water pump.
- Make sure that fire vehicles can reach your home.

Evacuation

Wildfires move fast. Be prepared to evacuate all family members and pets if fire nears or when you receive instructions from local officials. Plan several routes in case the fire blocks your escape route. Be ready to go. Park your car in an open space facing the direction of escape. Shut doors and roll up windows and leave the key in the ignition. *(See Evacuation, page 67.)*

DURING A WILDFIRE

- Be alert to changes in the speed and direction of fire and smoke.
- Listen to your battery-operated radio for reports and evacuation information.
- Wear protective clothing—sturdy shoes, cotton or woolen clothing, long pants, a long-sleeved shirt, gloves, and a handkerchief to protect your face.

If there is a fire in your area and you're sure you have time:

- Close all doors and windows inside your home to prevent draft.
- Close gas valves and turn off all pilot lights. Turn off propane tanks.
- Remove items from around the house—lawn furniture, tarps, and firewood. Move combustible furniture into the center of your home away from windows and sliding-glass doors. You can protect waterproofed valuables by placing them in a pool or pond.

- Connect your garden hose to the outside taps.
- Wet the roof. Use the hose or place lawn sprinklers on the roof.

If you're trapped:
WARNING: Don't try to outrun a wildfire!

Take shelter in a pool, pond, or river. Protect your head and body with wet clothing. If you can't find water, look for a cleared or rocky area; lie flat and cover up with wet clothing or earth. Breathe air close to the ground through a wet cloth to avoid smoke inhalation.

SMOKE

- Limit your exposure to smoke. Listen to news broadcasts and monitor local air-quality reports for health warnings about smoke.
- If advised to stay indoors, keep windows and doors shut if possible. Run air conditioner with the fresh-air intake closed.
- Paper dust masks are not sufficient to protect your lungs from smoke. The National Personal Protective Technology Laboratory and the National Institute for Occupational Safety and Health can provide a list of suitable protective masks.

AFTER A WILDFIRE

- Use caution when reentering a burned area. Hot spots can flare up without warning.
- Check roofs and attics and extinguish any lingering sparks or embers.

VOLCANOES

Although volcanic eruptions are among the most spectacular of natural disasters, fortunately they are among the rarest. The United States does have some significant areas of active volcanism, particularly the Pacific Northwest, Hawaii, and Alaska. In the event of a major eruption, volcanoes spew hot gases, ash, lava, and rock. Eruptions can hurl hot rocks (called bombs) for as far as 20 miles. Flash flooding, airborne ash, and toxic fumes can occur for miles around as the result of an eruption. The most common cause of death from a volcano is suffocation, and nonfatal health concerns include respiratory illness, burns, and injuries from falls and vehicle accidents caused by ash. Volcanic ash is gritty and abrasive and can cause respiratory conditions such as asthma, emphysema, and other chronic lung diseases. Infants and elderly people are particularly at risk. Volcanic gases such as carbon dioxide and sulfur dioxide usually blow away but can affect the health of people living close to the volcano. When warnings are heeded, however, the chances of adverse health effects from a volcanic eruption are very low.

IN THE EVENT OF A POTENTIAL ERUPTION

Geologists may be able to issue advance warning of a volcanic event:

- Monitor local radio and television broadcasts for information and emergency instructions.

- Follow the advice of local officials and obey evacuation orders immediately. Although it may seem safe to stay at home and wait out an eruption, doing so could be very dangerous.
- Develop an emergency communication plan for your family and maintain a disaster supply kit including goggles and a disposable breathing mask for each member of the household. N-95 disposable respirators (air-purifying respirators) can be purchased at hardware stores.

DURING AN ERUPTION

Outside:

- Avoid low-lying areas where poisonous gases can collect.
- Avoid streambeds and watch out for mud-flows.
- Cover your mouth and nose to protect yourself from volcanic ash.
- Keep skin covered to avoid irritation or burns; wear long-sleeved shirts and pants.
- Seek shelter indoors and close windows, doors, and dampers.
- Avoid driving in heavy ashfall; ash can clog engines and stall vehicles.

Inside:

- Turn off all fans and heating and air-conditioning systems.
- Bring pets and livestock into closed shelters.

- If your eyes, nose, and throat become irritated by volcanic gases, move away from the area immediately.

AFTER A VOLCANIC ERUPTION

- Listen to local news reports for information about air quality, drinking water, and roads.
- Turn off all heating and air-conditioning units and fans, and close windows and doors to keep ash and gases from getting into your house.
- Take steps to avoid contact with volcanic ashfall and windblown ash. Wear goggles to protect your eyes.
- Drink bottled water until your local water can be tested.
- Clear roofs of ash. Ash is very heavy and can cause buildings to collapse. Be very careful, volcanic ash can be slippery.

TERROR ATTACKS

The terrorist attacks of September 11 and other incidents worldwide raise concerns about the possibility of future attacks. There are steps you can take to prepare for a terrorist event. By making simple emergency preparations, you can reassure family members and exert a measure of control.

PREPARATION

Emergency Communications Plan

During a sudden local emergency like a terrorist attack, people flood the telephone lines with calls and overload cell phone service. In many cases, e-mail can get through when telephone calls cannot. During some emergencies, it may be easier to telephone an out-of-town number. Arrange for an out-of-town contact that members of your family can call or e-mail to check in should a disaster occur. Your contact should live far enough away to not be directly affected by an event in your area. Be sure that every member of your household knows the report-in number and other family contact information—e-mail addresses, telephone numbers (home, work, and cell).

Establish a meeting place

Agree upon a prearranged meeting place away from your home, where scattered family members can meet in the event of an evacuation or if your home area is affected.

School Emergency Plan

Find out about school emergency policies. Will

authorities hold children at school until a parent or designated adult can pick them up or plan to send them home on their own? Be sure that the school has updated information about how to reach parents and other caregivers to arrange for pickup. Find out what kind of authorization the school requires to release a child to someone you may designate to pick up your child.

Disaster Supplies Kit

Prepare a disaster supply kit in an easy-to-carry container. If you are forced to evacuate or are asked to "shelter in place," having some essential supplies on hand will make you and your family more comfortable. *(See Disaster Supply Kits, page 141.)*

DURING A TERROR INCIDENT

- Remain calm and be patient.
- Follow the advice of local emergency officials.
- Listen to radio or television broadcasts or the Emergency Broadcasting System for news and instructions.
- Follow basic disaster and first-aid procedures if you are in the affected area.
- Report in to your family contact number; avoid calling 911 unless the emergency is life threatening.
- Check on your neighbors, especially those who are elderly or disabled.

Evacuation

If local authorities ask you to leave your home, act immediately. Monitor radio or TV broadcasts for instructions from local emergency officials. Take your disaster supplies kit and follow basic evacuation procedures. *(See Disaster Supply Kits, page 141.)*

Shelter in Place:

If you are advised by local officials to "shelter in place," remain inside your home or office and protect yourself there. *(See Chemical and Radiological Emergencies, page 131.)*

AFTER A TERROR INCIDENT

- There may be significant casualties and damage to buildings and infrastructure.
- Public health resources in the affected area may be strained or even overwhelmed.
- Workplaces and schools may be closed, and there may be nighttime curfews and restrictions on local travel.

CHEMICAL, BIOLOGICAL, AND RADIOLOGICAL ATTACK

Many chemical agents cannot be seen or smelled. Protect yourself by observing the following: If a single person is choking or seizing, it is probable that this individual is having a heart attack or seizure. However, if several people are down, coughing, vomiting, or seizing, they could be reacting to a toxic substance. Also, birds and small animals are generally overcome more rapidly by poisons and toxic gasses than are humans. If large numbers of birds and small mammals are ill or dying in an area, a toxic substance may be present.

WARNING: Evacuate the area immediately and dial 911. Inform the operator that a hazardous gas may be present.

Indoors:

If an attack takes place indoors, exit the building quickly. Once outside, if you believe that you may have been exposed, don't be modest; shedding your clothes could save your life by removing as much as 80 percent of the toxic agent. Look for a source of water and thoroughly rinse any skin that may have been exposed. Remain calm and follow the instructions of emergency personnel.

Outdoors:

Quickly get a physical barrier between you and the toxic cloud. Get indoors and follow procedures for a chemical incident. *(See pages 130–134.)* Remain inside and monitor television or radio broadcasts. The Emergency Broadcast System will give instructions and notification when it is safe to go outside. Follow decontamination procedures. *(See Chemical and Radiological Emergencies, page 130.)*

Radiological Attack

If you learn that a radiological agent may have been released, remain indoors or get indoors right away; shut all windows and doors and turn off heating or air conditioning. Place a physical barrier between you and radioactive particles. A surgical mask or a respiratory protection mask rated for construction and laboratory use can help to screen out particulate matter that might be in the air. A mask must be fitted snugly over the nose and mouth.

CHEMICAL AND RADIOLOGICAL EMERGENCIES

A chemical or radiological emergency happens when a hazardous material is released into the environment. Chemicals are found everywhere. They are used to purify drinking water, as fertilizer, and as household cleaners. But many chemicals can be hazardous if released improperly. There is also a potential for harmful emissions from nuclear power facilities. Hazards can occur during production, storage, transportation, use, or disposal of both chemicals and radioactive materials.

TAKE PROTECTIVE MEASURES

Find out if there is a Local Emergency Planning Committee in your area and contact them to find out about local response and warning plans. If you live near a nuclear power facility, find out about regional warning systems and evacuation policies.

DURING AN EMERGENCY

- Stay away from the area of the accident to minimize the risk of contamination. Remember, some toxic chemicals and radiation are odorless and difficult to detect.
- In the event of a hazardous materials incident, listen to local radio or television broadcasts for information and instructions. You will be informed whether you need to evacuate or shelter in place.

EVACUATE

WARNING: If you are asked to evacuate, do so immediately!

Some kinds of radiological or chemical accidents may make staying put dangerous. In such cases, it may be safer for you to evacuate.

- Act quickly and follow the evacuation instructions of local emergency personnel—law enforcement, fire department, etc. Local authorities will provide special instructions to follow for a particular situation.

- Go immediately to an emergency shelter. Directions to the shelter should be provided by emergency personnel. If you have children in school, they will be sheltered there. Don't try to rush and pick them up at school, transporting them from the school can put them, and you, at increased risk.

SHELTER IN PLACE

Some kinds of radiological or chemical incidents may make going outdoors dangerous. Leaving the area might take too long and it may be safer for you to remain indoors. Shelter in place means to make a shelter out of the place you are in.

- Select a room in your home that has as few windows and doors as possible. A large room with a water supply is best. This room should be as high in the structure as possible to avoid gases that sink.

- Go inside as quickly as possible and go into a

preselected shelter room.

- Close and lock all exterior doors and windows. By locking, you will pull the door or window tighter and make a better seal.
- Turn off air conditioner or heater and all fans. Close vents, fireplace damper, and any other place that air can come in from.
- Tape plastic sheeting over all windows in the room. Use duct tape to make an unbroken seal around windows and doors. Stuff sealing material around pipes and other openings; tape over any vents, electrical outlets, or other openings.
- Turn on the radio or TV for emergency information and public safety announcements. An announcement will be made when it is safe to leave the shelter.
- Drink only stored water, not water from the tap. *(See Water, page 34.)*

Outside

WARNING: Stay upstream, uphill, and upwind!

Try to go at least a half-mile (8 to 10 blocks) from the danger area. Avoid any spilled liquids, particles, or chemical vapors. If you are in a motor vehicle, keep the windows and vents closed and shut off the air conditioner and heater. Stop and seek shelter in a permanent building if possible.

- If you are away from your home shelter-in-place location when a chemical event occurs, follow the instructions of local emergency authorities to find the nearest shelter. If your children are at school, they will be sheltered there. Unless you are instructed to do so, do not try to get to the school to bring your children home. Transporting them from the school will put them, and you, at increased risk.

AFTER A CHEMICAL OR RADIOLOGICAL EMERGENCY

- When you leave a shelter, follow the instructions of your local emergency officials. Return home only when authorities say it is safe and avoid contact with any remaining contaminants.
- Open windows and ventilate your house.
- Act quickly if you have come in contact with or have been exposed to hazardous materials. Follow decontamination instructions from local authorities and seek medical treatment for any unusual symptoms.

Decontamination

In the event that you come into contact with hazardous materials, it may make be necessary for you to remove and dispose of your clothing right away and wash yourself to remove or reduce contamination. If you think that you may have been exposed to a toxic substance, don't be modest, getting out of contaminated clothing could save your life. Many chemical agents are absorbed rapidly through the skin. Decontamination should be carried out within minutes of exposure. Act quickly and follow the instructions of local emergency officials.

- Remove your clothing: Quickly take off clothing that has been contaminated by contact with dangerous chemicals. Don't pull contaminated clothing over your head, cut it away.
- Wash any chemicals or particles from your skin as quickly as possible, using large amounts of soap and water. If your eyes have been affected, flush with plain water for 10 to 15 minutes. Remove contaminated contact lenses and discard them; don't put them back in. Wash eyeglasses with soap and water.
- Dispose of your clothes: After bathing, place your clothing and anything else that has come in contact with the contaminated clothing in a plastic bag. Avoid touching contaminated clothing. Wear rubber gloves or use tongs, tool handles, sticks, etc., which should also be placed in the plastic bag. If you wear contacts, put them in the plastic bag, too. Seal the bag and place it inside a second plastic bag. Health department or emergency personnel will arrange for further disposal.
- Dress in clothing that has not been contaminated. Clothing stored in drawers or closets is probably safe.

10. PETS

Pets need protection in the event of a natural disaster and an evacuaion. It is generally not safe to leave them behind, since they depend on you for their survival. Local animal control agencies can inform you about community resources for protecting pets in an emergency. Be aware that Red Cross and other shelters may not be able to accept animals.

In a disaster situation, your pet may be frightened and confused and will need comfort. Signs of stress include loss of appetite, aggressiveness, nervousness, diarrhea, and changes in sleep habits.

PLAN AHEAD
- Ask relatives and friends outside of your area if they would be willing to keep your pets in the event of an emergency evacuation. Check with motels and hotels where you might stay about their pet policies.
- License your dogs and cats. ID tags will help locate and recover them if they get lost.
- Keep vaccinations current (rabies, distemper/parvo and respiratory complex, etc.), especially if you expect to board your pet. Keep documentation together with other records.
- Take photographs of your pets and keep the

photos with important documents. Be sure to include any distinguishing marks. These pictures can help you recover a lost pet.

- You may not be home when a disaster strikes; make arrangements with a neighbor to take your pets to a designated location.
- Prepare a pet disaster kit.
- Keep a leash handy and get your pet used to it.
- Own a pet carrier that can contain your pet (large enough for the pet to stand up and turn around in) and also fit into your vehicle.

DURING A DISASTER

- Confine your pets in easy-to-clean areas such as bathrooms, kitchen, or utility rooms.
- Check collars for tags and make sure they are securely attached. Obtain extra ID tags with your name and address. You can also mark collars, using indelible ink, with the phone number and address of temporary shelters.

Evacuating Birds, Reptiles, and Small Mammals

Transport birds and lizards in a secure cage or carrier. Wrap the cage in a blanket in cool weather. In hot weather, use a plant mister to cool them down.

- Snakes can be transported in a pillowcase.
- Small mammals can be transported in secure carriers along with food, water bottles, and bedding materials.

NOTE: If you have time, you can make a temporary warmer for temperature-sensitive pets by heating a sock filled with uncooked rice in the microwave (heat on high for 2 minutes). Make sure to test the temperature!

If you must leave a pet behind:

- Bring your pet inside. NEVER leave your pet outside or tied up during a hurricane.
- Secure your pets in a room inside the house in an area away from windows. Don't confine incompatible pets together! Make sure your pet can get onto a high area, in case flooding occurs.
- Leave water in sturdy, nonspill containers or in the bathtub if it is accessible.
- Leave out only dry pet foods in sturdy containers. You might want to consider selecting a food that is not a favorite of your pet. This will keep them from overeating. Use special food dispensers for birds; birds must eat daily to survive.

AFTER A DISASTER

Be careful about allowing your pet outdoors alone or off-leash. Familiar scents and landmarks may be absent and your pet could easily get confused and become lost. Downed power lines, fallen trees, debris, and contaminated water could present real dangers to your pet.

11. ANIMAL AND INSECT HAZARDS

Many wild animals, like other residents in the aftermath of a natural disaster, may become displaced and left homeless. As a result, it is not surprising to find these animals seeking shelter and food in areas close to people. Damaged structures can attract snakes due to the many accessible entrances, and displaced snakes may also be found under scattered debris. In the aftermath of a natural disaster:

- Avoid wild or stray animals.
- If possible, call local authorities to handle or retrieve animals.
- Dispose of dead animals as soon as possible. Follow the recommendations of your local animal control authority.
- Remove debris that might provide shelter for snakes, rats, and mice.
- Clean up any food sources, animal carcasses, and garbage that might attract rats as soon as possible.

SNAKES
Outdoors:
- Learn to recognize nonvenomous and venomous snakes. There are many books available on snake identification or you can contact your state wildlife agency.

- In the event of a flood, snakes may be swimming in the water to get to higher ground.
- If you encounter a snake, back away from it slowly and do not touch it; step back and let it proceed on its way.
- Be careful where you put your hands and feet when removing or cleaning debris. Try not to put your fingers under items that you plan to move.
- Never step over logs or other obstacles unless you can see the other side.

Indoors:

- Nonvenomous snakes can be pinned down with a stick or removed by scooping them up with a shovel. If you don't want to move the snake yourself, contact a wildlife officer.
- If you need to kill a venomous snake, club it with a garden hoe, long stick, or other tool. Never try to kill a venomous snake with something that is shorter than the snake's striking range—usually a little less than half of its total length.
- If you are bitten by a venomous snake, don't try to treat the bite yourself. Seek medical attention immediatly.
  - Try to see and remember the color and shape of the snake to help with treatment.
  - Keep a bitten person still and calm to slow down the spread of venom.
  - Lay the person down with the bite below the level of the heart.

MOSQUITOES

Rain and flooding following a hurricane or severe storm may lead to an increase in numbers of mosquitoes. In most cases, mosquitoes will simply be a nuisance but some carry communicable diseases such as West Nile virus.

- Listen to radio and TV news broadcasts for warnings of mosquito-borne diseases issued by local, state, and federal public health authorities.
- Wearing long-sleeved shirts, long pants, socks and hats decreases the area of exposed skin. Apply insect repellents that contain DEET or Picaridin. Always follow the manufacturer's directions and be careful when using DEET on small children.
- Repair or install screens on dwelling places.
- Control mosquito populations by draining all standing water left outdoors in open containers.
- Many mosquito species are most active at dawn and dusk. You can reduce risk of exposure by avoiding outdoor activity at these times.

12. DISASTER SUPPLY KITS

A disaster can happen anytime and anywhere and when it does, you may not have much time to respond. A hazardous material spill on the highway could require a quick getaway, or a winter storm could keep your family shut in at home for days. A disaster such as a hurricane, flood, tornado, or earthquake could cut off basic services to your home, and electricity, water, gas, and telephones may be out for several days. An important part of your disaster readiness plan should be to review potential disaster situations that might occur in your region and assemble the supplies you might need after a disaster strikes.

At the least, you should have:
- ❑ Flashlight and extra batteries
- ❑ Portable, battery-powered radio or TV and extra batteries
- ❑ Pocketknife or knife/multi-tool
- ❑ Heavy-duty (contractor weight) plastic trash bags
- ❑ One-gallon water container
- ❑ A "survival" or "space" blanket
- ❑ Copies of family records and documents
- ❑ Matches in a waterproof container

BASIC DISASTER SUPPLY KIT

Gather the supplies that you and your family will need if you remain in place during and after a disaster. Store the supplies you most likely will need for an evacuation in an easy-to-carry, water-proof container. Label it clearly and keep it in a designated and easy-to-reach location. Be sure the entire family knows where it is located.

Containers

- Covered plastic or metal trash container
- Plastic storage container with sealable lid
- Large duffel bag
- Camping backpack
- Cargo container that will fit on the roof of your vehicle

Maintaining Your Kit: It is just as important to maintain your kits so they are safe and ready to use.

- Store items in airtight plastic bags to help protect them from damage.
- Store canned foods in a dry, cool place. Store boxed food in tightly closed plastic or metal containers to protect from pests.
- Replace stored food and water supplies every six months. Write the date on food and water containers when you store them. Place new items at the back of the storage area and older ones in the front.
- Replace batteries at least once a year.
- Put your entire disaster supplies kit in one or two easy-to-carry containers.

CONTENTS

The following items are recommended for inclusion in your disaster supplies kit:

Water *(See Water, page 34.)*

Keep a three-day supply of water. Store one gallon of water per person per day—two quarts for drinking, two quarts for food preparation and sanitation. Heat and physical activity can double the amount needed. Children, nursing mothers, and sick people will need additional water. Store your three-day supply in a convenient place. Include any items needed for water purification.

Food *(See Food Safety, page 42.)*

Three-day supply of nonperishable food. Remember to store nonperishable foods for your pets.

Clothing and Bedding

- ❏ One complete change of clothing and footwear per person
- ❏ Socks
- ❏ Underwear (thermal underwear for cold weather)
- ❏ Hat or cap and gloves
- ❏ Sturdy shoes or boots
- ❏ Rain gear
- ❏ Sunglasses
- ❏ Blankets or sleeping bags for each person
- ❏ "Survival" or "space" blankets
- ❏ Jacket or coat

REMEMBER: When updating your kits, be sure to account for variables such as change of seasons and growing children.

EMERGENCY SUPPLIES AND TOOLS

Basic Supplies

❏ Portable, battery-powered radio or TV and extra batteries (An NOAA Weather Radio is a good addition.)
❏ Flashlight and extra batteries
❏ Matches in a waterproof container
❏ Tools: utility knife, shut-off wrench, pliers, shovel, ax or hatchet, crowbar
❏ Duct tape and scissors
❏ Plastic sheeting or tarps
❏ Heavy-duty plastic zip ties
❏ Rope or cord
❏ Contractor-weight plastic trash bags (These are handy for a wide variety of uses from storage to improvised rain gear.)
❏ Fire extinguisher
❏ Work gloves
❏ Needles and thread
❏ Paper, pens, and pencils
❏ Emergency flares and whistle

Kitchen Items

❏ Small cooking stove and a supply of cooking fuel (if food must be cooked)
❏ Cooking utensils
❏ Manual can opener
❏ All-purpose knife
❏ Mess kits, or a supply of disposable plastic eating utensils
❏ Aluminum foil and plastic wrap
❏ Resealable plastic bags

- ❏ Sugar, salt, pepper
- ❏ Coffee filters (for filtering water)

Sanitation and Hygiene Supplies

- ❏ Washcloth and towel
- ❏ Towelettes, soap, waterless hand sanitizer
- ❏ Toothpaste, toothbrushes
- ❏ Shampoo, comb, and brush
- ❏ Razor, shaving cream
- ❏ Contact lens solution
- ❏ Feminine supplies
- ❏ Sunscreen, lip balm
- ❏ Insect repellent
- ❏ Toilet paper
- ❏ Heavy-duty plastic garbage bags and ties for personal sanitation uses
- ❏ Medium-sized plastic bucket (5-gallon) with tight lid
- ❏ Disinfectant
- ❏ Household chlorine bleach (used for treating water and making disinfectants)
- ❏ Mirror
- ❏ Small shovel

Special Items

- ❏ Prescription medications and copies of prescriptions
- ❏ Spare eyeglasses and contact lens solution
- ❏ Hearing-aid batteries
- ❏ Denture needs
- ❏ Diapers, infant formula, and bottles
- ❏ Nonelectronic entertainment (games, books, and cards)

Identification, Money, and Keys

- ❏ Extra keys for house, car, boat, etc.
- ❏ Reserve supply of cash and coins
- ❏ Emergency contact list and phone numbers
- ❏ Copies of personal identification (driver's license, passport, etc.)
- ❏ List of credit card numbers
- ❏ Map of the area (for locating shelters) and phone numbers of places you could go

Copies of Important Documents

(Keep in a watertight container.)

- ❏ Birth and marriage certificates
- ❏ Social Security cards
- ❏ Passports
- ❏ Immunization records
- ❏ Wills and deeds
- ❏ Insurance papers and policies
- ❏ Inventory of household goods
- ❏ Bank and credit card account numbers
- ❏ Stocks, bonds, and contracts

BASIC FIRST-AID KIT

- ❏ First-aid manual (available from your local American Red Cross)
- ❏ Sterile adhesive bandages (Band-Aids) in assorted sizes
- ❏ Latex gloves (2 pairs)
- ❏ 2-inch sterile gauze pads (4-6)
- ❏ 4-inch sterile gauze pads (4-6)
- ❏ Triangular bandages (3)

- ❏ 2-inch sterile roller bandages (3 rolls)
- ❏ 3-inch sterile roller bandages (3 rolls)
- ❏ Hypoallergenic adhesive tape
- ❏ Scissors
- ❏ Tweezers
- ❏ Needle
- ❏ Antiseptic and alcohol wipes
- ❏ Antibiotic ointment
- ❏ Hydrogen peroxide
- ❏ Thermometer
- ❏ Assorted sizes of safety pins
- ❏ Tube of petroleum jelly or other lubricant
- ❏ Waterless hand sanitizer
- ❏ Sunscreen

Nonprescription Drugs

- ❏ Aspirin or non-aspirin pain reliever
- ❏ Antidiarrheal medication
- ❏ Antacid (for upset stomach)
- ❏ Laxative
- ❏ Vitamins
- ❏ Infant medicines (for children under 2 years of age)
- ❏ Allergy medicines (for persons with severe allergies)
- ❏ Syrup of ipecac (Use to induce vomiting if advised by the poison control center.)
- ❏ Activated charcoal (Use if advised by the poison control center.)
- ❏ Ask your physician or pharmacist about acquiring and storing a supply of prescription medications.

EVACUATION KIT

- ❏ Water—3 gallons per person
- ❏ Food—3-day supply, nonperishable
- ❏ First-aid kit
- ❏ Eating utensils
- ❏ Battery-powered radio and extra batteries
- ❏ Flashlight and extra batteries
- ❏ Cash or traveler's checks
- ❏ Nonelectric can opener, utility knife
- ❏ Toilet paper, premoistened wipes
- ❏ Soap, liquid detergent
- ❏ Personal hygiene items
- ❏ Prescription and nonprescription medications
- ❏ At least one complete change of clothing and footwear per person
- ❏ Sturdy shoes or work boots
- ❏ Blankets or sleeping bag per person
- ❏ List of important telephone numbers
- ❏ Important family documents (in a waterproof container)
- ❏ An inventory of household goods
- ❏ Infant supplies: formula, diapers, bottles, powdered milk, medications, etc.

CAR KIT

You should keep a smaller version of the disaster supply kit in the trunk of each of your cars. In case you are stranded, your kit should contain food, water, first-aid supplies, flares, jumper cables, and seasonal supplies.

- ❏ Water—several bottles of water
- ❏ High-calorie nonperishable food (If you include cans, remember a manual can opener.)
- ❏ Cell phone charger
- ❏ Road maps and compass
- ❏ Battery-powered radio and extra batteries
- ❏ Flashlight and extra batteries
- ❏ First-aid kit and any necessary medications
- ❏ Extra clothing including footwear, hat, and gloves
- ❏ Rain gear
- ❏ Blankets (special "survival" or "space" blankets are best) or sleeping bags
- ❏ Rags or paper towels
- ❏ Road flares
- ❏ Fire extinguisher
- ❏ Waterproof matches
- ❏ Pocketknife
- ❏ Small tool kit, pliers, wrenches, and a screwdriver
- ❏ Plastic bags for sanitation
- ❏ Jumper cables
- ❏ Tow chain
- ❏ Shovel and ax or hatchet
- ❏ Canned tire sealant with compressed air (for emergency tire repair)

Winter

- ❏ Ice scraper and brush
- ❏ Brightly colored cloth to tie to the antenna
- ❏ Sand or cat litter, tire chains or traction mats
- ❏ Road salt

❑ Extra clothing—caps, mittens, overshoes, etc.
❑ Additional blankets or sleeping bags, or
   newspaper to use as insulation

PET EMERGENCY KIT

Place your supplies in a labeled plastic container.

❑ License and identification for your pet!
   Keep a collar with a current license on your
   pet and store an extra collar in your kit.
❑ A three-day supply of food and water. Buy
   food in the smallest possible cans to avoid
   spoilage. (Include a manual can opener.)
❑ Food and water dishes
❑ Necessary medications
❑ Copies of medical and immunization
   records stored in a waterproof container
❑ Sturdy leashes/harness for each animal
❑ Pooper-scooper or supply of cat litter and
   plastic bags for disposing of waste
❑ Carrier or crate for each animal with a
   secure locking device
❑ Disinfectant cleaner and paper towels
❑ Favorite toys and bedding
❑ Recent photographs of your pet for
   identification purposes

13. EMERGENCY AND DISASTER RESOURCES

INSURANCE, GRANT, AND LOAN PROGRAMS

The federal government in cooperation with state authorities and private firms offers a range of disaster insurance, loan and grant programs. Contact FEMA offices for detailed information concerning the provisions of these programs. In all federally sponsored programs, the loss must have been suffered during a recognized (proclaimed by the president) natural disaster. Be sure to find out the provisions of all government assistance programs to determine your own possible financial liability.

INSURANCE

The National Flood Insurance Program

The National Flood Insurance Program (NFIP) is administered by the Federal Emergency Management Agency (FEMA). It is a cooperative effort between the federal government and private homeowner's insurance companies. Under federal regulations, private insurance companies receive a percentage of the premium payments and pass the remainder to the NFIP. In the event of a loss, the private insurance companies are paid an additional 3 percent of the loss. Under this system, FEMA flood insurance representatives are government contractors rather than officials of the U.S. government. Federal regulations call for the insurance companies to make adjustments in accordance with their standard policies.

LOANS

- **Home Mortgage Insurance:**
  The Department of Housing and Urban Development (HUD), working through approved lenders, offers mortgage insurance for individuals and families whose homes were destroyed or significantly damaged by a presidentially declared natural disaster. The program assists individuals in purchasing a new home or rebuilding their old one.
- **Small Business Administration:**
  Disaster relief loans are available for qualifying businesses.

FEMA GRANTS

Federal Assistance to Individual and House-holds Program (IHP)

A federal and state program administered by FEMA that offers grants for housing assistance and other needs. The grants cover only disaster-related necessary expenses and serious needs, such as transportation, personal property, and medical, dental, and funeral expenses.

FEMA TEMPORARY HOUSING PROGRAM

- **Mortgage and Rental Assistance Program:** Provides assistance to individuals or families who have received notice of eviction or foreclosure due to financial hardship caused by a disaster.
- **Rental Assistance:** Available to homeowners or renters whose dwelling is unlivable as a direct result of a disaster.
- **Minimal Repair Program:** Provides money for primary residences which may have sustained minor damage but are unlivable as a direct result of a disaster.

EMERGENCY ASSISTANCE

Emergency Food Coupons

May be made available to disaster victims under a program administered by the U.S. Department of Agriculture and the state authorities.

UNEMPLOYMENT

Disaster Unemployment Assistance

People who lose their jobs due to a disaster may apply for Disaster Unemployment Assistance (DUA) to receive weekly benefits if they are not eligible for regular unemployment insurance compensation.

14. NATIONAL EMERGENCY RESOURCES

AMERICAN RED CROSS

American Red Cross hotline for information on personal and family disaster preparedness, international humanitarian assistance, services to the military, and all Red Cross services.

American Red Cross National Headquarters
2025 E Street, NW, Washington, D.C. 20006
Phone: (202) 303-4498 or 1-866-GET-INFO
(1-866-438-4636) www.redcross.org

Donations can be made online or by calling
1-800-HELP-NOW (1-800-435-7669)

CENTERS FOR DISEASE CONTROL AND PREVENTION (CDC)

Public Health Emergency Preparedness and Response
www.bt.cdc.gov

CITIZENCORPS.GOV

Created to help coordinate volunteer activities for emergency preparedness.
www.citizencorps.gov

DEPARTMENT OF HEALTH AND HUMAN SERVICES

Disasters and Emergencies
http://hhs.gov/emergency

DISASTER HELP
Information and services relating to disaster management: preparedness, response, recovery, and migration.

https://disasterhelp.gov/portal/jhtml/index.jhtml

ENVIRONMENTAL PROTECTION AGENCY
Emergency Preparedness

www.epa.gov/ebtpages

FEDERAL CITIZEN INFORMATION CENTER (FCIC)
Call the Federal Citizen Information Center for answers about federal agencies, programs, benefits, or services.

1-800-FED-INFO (1-800-333-4636)

FEDERAL EMERGENCY MANAGEMENT AGENCY (FEMA)
www.fema.gov

1-800-621-FEMA (1-800-621-3362)

FIRSTGOV.GOV
The official web portal of the U.S. federal government

www.firstgov.gov

NATIONAL WEATHER SERVICE
National Oceanic and Atmospheric Administration (NOAA)

www.weather.gov

NATIONAL FLOOD INSURANCE PROGRAM

Contact to determine flood risk for homes or businesses located in the United States. Can help locate an insurance agent who sells flood insurance in your area.

www.floodsmart.gov/floodsmart/pages/index.jsp

SMALL BUSINESS ADMINISTRATION

Small Business Administration
3rd Street, SW, Washington, D.C. 20416
202-205-6734 www.sba.gov

U.S. DEPARTMENT OF HOMELAND SECURITY

Emergency preparedness guidance from the U.S. Department of Homeland Security lists and explains specific threats and responses.

www.dhs.gov or www.ready.gov
1-800-BE-READY (1-800-237-3239)
Operator: 202-282-8000

U.S. GEOLOGICAL SURVEY (USGS)

Information on the landscape, our natural resources, and natural hazards that could threaten us.

www.usgs.gov

EMERGENCY CONTACTS

LIFE-THREATENING EMERGENCY—DIAL 911
Other local emergency number: _____
Police (non-emergency): _____
Fire (non-emergency): _____

LOCAL CONTACT
Name: _____
Phone: Day _____ Evening _____

OUT-OF-REGION CONTACT
Name: _____
Phone: Day _____ Evening _____
Email: _____

NEIGHBORHOOD MEETING PLACE
Where: _____
Phone: _____

OUT OF THE NEIGHBORHOOD MEETING PLACE
Where: _____
Address: _____
_____
Phone: _____

SCHOOL(S)
Name: _____
_____
Address: _____
_____
Phone: _____
Evacuation Location: _____
_____

DOCTOR(S)
Name: _____
Phone: _____
Veterinarian: _____
Phone: _____

FAMILY NUMBERS
Name: _____ Phone: _____
Name: _____ Phone: _____
Name: _____ Phone: _____
Name: _____ Phone: _____
Name: _____ Phone: _____
Name: _____ Phone: _____

INDEX